*Tim Huxley and
Susan Willett*

**Arming East Asia**

*Adelphi Paper* 329

Oxford University Press, Great Clarendon Street, Oxford OX2 6DP
Oxford New York
Athens Auckland Bangkok Bombay Calcutta Cape Town
Dar es Salaam Delhi Florence Hong Kong Istanbul Karachi
Kuala Lumpur Madras Madrid Melbourne Mexico City
Nairobi Paris Singapore Taipei Tokyo Toronto
and associated companies in
Berlin Ibadan

Oxford is a trade mark of Oxford University Press

Published in the United States
by Oxford University Press Inc., New York

© The International Institute for Strategic Studies 1999

**First published** July 1999 by **Oxford University Press** for
**The International Institute for Strategic Studies**
23 Tavistock Street, London WC2E 7NQ

**Director** John Chipman
**Editor** Gerald Segal
**Assistant Editor** Matthew Foley
**Project Manager, Design and Production** Mark Taylor

British Library Cataloguing in Publication Data
Data available

Library of Congress Cataloguing in Publication Data

**ISBN** 0-19-922432-3
**ISSN** 0567-932x

_contents_

*map & tables*

| | |
|---|---|
| ADB | Asian Development Bank |
| AEW | airborne early warning |
| AIA | Aerospace Industries Association (US) |
| AIDC | Aero Industry Development Centre (Taiwan) |
| AMRAAM | advanced medium-range air-to-air missile |
| ASEAN | Association of South-East Asian Nations |
| $C^4$ | command, control, communications and computer-processing |
| COCOM | Coordinating Committee for Multinational Export Controls |
| COSTIND | Commission for Science, Technology and Industry for National Defence (China) |
| CSIST | Chung Shan Institute of Science and Technology (Taiwan) |
| DESO | Defence Export Services Organisation (UK) |
| DMZ | demilitarised zone (Korean Peninsula) |
| EU | European Union |
| FMS | Foreign Military Sales (US) |
| FPDA | Five Power Defence Arrangements |
| GDP | gross domestic product |
| GED | General Equipment Department (China) |
| ICBM | intercontinental ballistic missile |

| | |
|---|---|
| IDF | Indigenous Defence Fighter (Taiwan) |
| IMF | International Monetary Fund |
| ISR | intelligence collection, surveillance and reconnaissance |
| JDA | Japan Defense Agency |
| MoU | Memorandum of Understanding |
| NGO | non-governmental organisation |
| NMD | national missile defence |
| OSCE | Organisation for Security and Cooperation in Europe |
| PLA | People's Liberation Army (China) |
| R&D | research and development |
| RMA | 'revolution in military affairs' |
| SAM | surface-to-air missile |
| SLBM | submarine-launched ballistic missile |
| TMD | theatre missile defence |
| UAV | unmanned aerial vehicle |
| WMD | weapons of mass destruction |

*introduction*

East Asia has been more peaceful during the 1990s than at almost
any other time in the twentieth century. Nonetheless, the region's
military spending and arms procurement have grown rapidly, and
its defence industries have expanded. The economic crisis which
began in July 1997 has forced some regional states to reduce their
defence spending, but most have remained committed to boosting
their military capabilities. East Asian governments and most aca-
demics argue that regional states have simply 'modernised' their
armed forces, implying mere upgrading or replacement of existing
equipment. But many have in fact developed new capabilities which
go far beyond simple modernisation by seeking to increase mobility,
firepower and the ability to locate targets. The emphasis has been on
conventional weapons, but in North-east Asia there has also been a
significant non-conventional dimension to military programmes.
This has involved developing and deploying nuclear weapons and
associated delivery systems.

Using the term 'arms race' to describe these developments
suggests an intensity of competition that has been largely absent.
The military programmes of pairs of states, notably China and
Taiwan and the two Koreas, have influenced one another. Less
intense competition has taken place between Japan and South Korea,
Japan and China, and combinations of South-east Asian states such
as Malaysia and Singapore. However, while threat perceptions have
been important in influencing levels of defence spending and
procurement, other factors have also been relevant:

- increased state funds as a result of rapid economic growth before the 1997 crisis;
- the influence of the armed forces on political and economic decision-making in some East Asian states;
- internal security concerns, particularly in South-east Asia;
- military modernisation and the development of defence industries as part of overall national modernisation and industrialisation;
- national prestige, in relation both to neighbouring states and to domestic audiences;
- uncertainty over the region's strategic future;
- the increasing salience of maritime security issues; and
- pressure from arms suppliers.

The economic crisis has reduced procurement funds in some states, and slowed national modernisation and defence industrialisation. It has also contributed to domestic political change, in some cases reducing the military's role in decision-making. But other influences – the region's uncertain strategic future, maritime security issues and major internal security concerns – remain relevant.

While military developments in East Asia in the 1990s may not amount to an arms race, they do have important implications for suppliers of defence equipment, for arms control and for regional stability. East Asia became an increasingly important market for US, European and other outside suppliers, notably from Russia and Israel, as their domestic markets contracted with the end of the Cold War. Although US suppliers have remained pre-eminent, competition has increased and others have won significant contracts. European firms, notably from France and the UK, have often supplied equipment unavailable from the US. Russia has regained its role as a significant defence exporter to the region, mainly because of its willingness to supply China, which has been subject to Western arms embargoes since 1989. To operate successfully in East Asia, suppliers have had to adopt increasingly sophisticated methods, for example providing economic compensation (offsets) to purchasing countries, including the transfer of technology, and by accepting unorthodox payment methods.

These developments raise questions over whether arms-control measures can check the flow of conventional military

**Map 1** *East Asia*

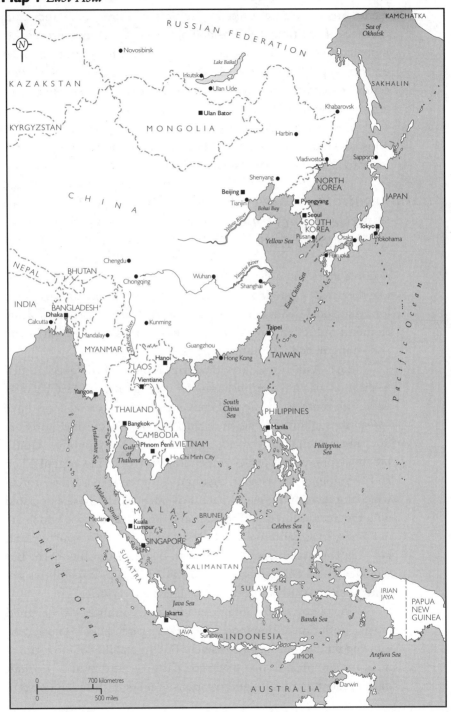

equipment and defence technology to East Asia. Supplier governments are more interested in promoting, rather than reducing, transfers of equipment and technology; East Asian governments are more concerned with modernising, rather than limiting, their defence capabilities. There is therefore little prospect that arms control will have more than a marginal impact on the conventional arms trade with East Asia.

East Asian states have not depended entirely on imported arms, and most have improved the capabilities of their own defence industries in the 1990s. Greater national self-sufficiency in arms production is an oft-stated goal, but the continued dependence of East Asian industries on foreign technology and know-how reflects their limited capacities, even in the region's more technologically advanced states. These deficiencies, together with changing economic and political conditions, have forced regional defence industries to restructure by diversifying into civilian production, and through commercialisation, privatisation and strengthened international links.

*arms control will have little impact on the arms trade*

East Asia's military modernisation and defence industrialisation also have implications for the regional military balance. Although more sophisticated conventional weapon systems have spread throughout the region during the 1990s, acquiring hardware does not automatically mean greater military capabilities. Qualitative factors related to personnel, logistics, doctrine, organisation and technology are vital in distinguishing between armed forces which are developing real capabilities, particularly those associated with the 'revolution in military affairs' (RMA), and those which are not doing so. Qualitative weaknesses and a lack of resources limit how far East Asian armed forces can benefit from the RMA. But regional states deploying even partial RMA-type capabilities are gaining military advantages over potential adversaries.

The region's most militarily advanced countries – US-aligned Japan, South Korea, Singapore and Taiwan – are unlikely to use their growing military means aggressively. But the stability of the regional military balance is not assured. Chinese and North Korean development of missiles and weapons of mass destruction (WMD), together with Beijing's nascent RMA-type capabilities, could erode the conventional military advantages of the US and its regional allies. There are thus good reasons to continue building a regional security architecture, with rules-based institutions. Prevailing domestic and regional political conditions may not, however, allow this endeavour to succeed.

## chapter 1

# Defence Spending and Economic Crisis

Defence spending in East Asia grew by some 40% between 1985 and 1996, though some states increased their spending more quickly than others, and some geared expenditure to their economic perform-ance.[1] The economic crisis which began in July 1997 has reduced spending in the region's hardest-hit countries, leading to the cancellation or postponement of major procurement programmes.

## Defence Spending in South-East Asia

South-east Asian governments spend much less on defence than their North-east Asian counterparts. In 1997, for example, South Korea's defence spending of $14.8 billion was almost as large as the combined total spending ($16.1bn) of Indonesia, Malaysia, Singa-pore and Thailand. Nevertheless, the dollar value of defence spending grew significantly across the sub-region between 1985 and 1996. In Indonesia, expenditure increased by 44%, in Malaysia by 47%, by 61% in Myanmar, 65% in Thailand, and by 125% and 144% in the Philippines and Singapore respectively.[2] Vietnam was the only major South-east Asian state not to increase its defence spending substantially; in fact, the withdrawal of Soviet aid caused it to fall by some 70%.[3] Since mid-1997, the economic crisis has reduced growth and cut state revenues, forcing several South-east Asian govern-ments to curtail their defence spending for the duration of the downturn. The depreciation of local currencies against the dollar has substantially reduced the international purchasing power of remaining procurement funds.

**Table 1** *East Asian Defence Spending,*
*1985, 1993–1998*

| (1997 US$m) | 1985 | 1993 | 1994 | 1995 | 1996 | 1997 | 1998 |
|---|---|---|---|---|---|---|---|
| China | 28,273 | 29,909 | 30,412 | 34,345 | 36,176 | 36,551 | 36,709 |
| Indonesia | 3,334 | 3,662 | 3,608 | 4,592 | 4,797 | 4,812 | 4,894 |
| Japan | 30,612 | 45,569 | 49,003 | 52,378 | 45,502 | 40,891 | 36,990 |
| South Korea | 8,962 | 13,097 | 13,386 | 15,030 | 16,172 | 14,768 | 9,652 |
| Malaysia | 2,513 | 3,172 | 3,301 | 3,665 | 3,695 | 3,377 | 3,222 |
| Myanmar | 1,252 | 1,747 | 1,914 | 1,961 | 2,012 | 2,167 | 2,059 |
| Philippines | 675 | 1,165 | 1,255 | 1,420 | 1,520 | 1,422 | 973 |
| Singapore | 1,692 | 2,929 | 3,276 | 4,141 | 4,258 | 4,624 | 4,276 |
| Taiwan | 9,171 | 13,149 | 12,058 | 13,708 | 13,868 | 13,657 | 13,887 |
| Thailand | 2,669 | 3,530 | 3,886 | 4,179 | 4,939 | 3,326 | 2,041 |
| Vietnam | 3,418 | 786 | 1,043 | 949 | 970 | 990 | 735 |

**Source** IISS, June 1999

In Thailand, economic problems had affected defence budgets even before the crisis. In mid-1996 and April 1997, the government's concerns over a ballooning current-account deficit led Bangkok to freeze spending at 1995 levels, forcing the procurement of submarines and a communications satellite to be postponed.[4] Following the crisis, more stringent constraints were imposed. Austerity measures required by the International Monetary Fund (IMF)'s recovery package cut 24bn baht from the B105bn defence budget planned for the 1998 fiscal year, commencing in October 1997.[5] The 1998 procurement budget fell to a mere $200 million; equipment already bought had to be paid for at unexpectedly unfavourable exchange rates, preventing little new procurement beyond spare parts.[6] After protracted negotiations, the US in early 1998 allowed Thailand to cancel its 1996 order for eight F/A-18 fighter aircraft, without incurring financial penalties beyond the $75m down payment already made.[7] Plans to buy armoured vehicles, transport helicopters and aircraft, airborne early warning (AEW) aircraft, air-defence radar and in-flight refuelling tankers were deferred, as were plans to upgrade F-16 fighters.[8] Payment for even minor purchases, such as Israeli unmanned aerial vehicles (UAVs), was rescheduled.[9]

**Table 2** *East Asian Defence Spending as a Percentage of GDP,
1985, 1993–1998*

|  | 1985 | 1993 | 1994 | 1995 | 1996 | 1997 | 1998 |
|---|---|---|---|---|---|---|---|
| China | 7.9 | 5.3 | 5.3 | 5.9 | 5.7 | 5.7 | 5.3 |
| Indonesia | 2.8 | 2.1 | 2.2 | 2.2 | 2.1 | 2.2 | 2.3 |
| Japan | 1.0 | 1.0 | 1.0 | 1.0 | 1.0 | 1.0 | 1.0 |
| South Korea | 5.1 | 3.6 | 3.3 | 3.4 | 3.7 | 3.3 | 2.3 |
| Malaysia | 5.6 | 4.5 | 4.3 | 4.5 | 4.2 | 3.4 | 3.2 |
| Myanmar | 5.1 | 7.0 | 7.5 | 7.5 | 7.6 | 7.7 | 6.8 |
| Philippines | 1.4 | 2.0 | 2.0 | 2.2 | 2.2 | 1.9 | 1.5 |
| Singapore | 6.7 | 4.6 | 4.3 | 4.9 | 4.7 | 4.8 | 4.4 |
| Taiwan | 7.0 | 5.4 | 4.7 | 5.1 | 4.8 | 4.6 | 4.5 |
| Thailand | 5.0 | 2.6 | 2.5 | 2.6 | 2.9 | 2.2 | 1.5 |
| Vietnam | 19.4 | 3.9 | 4.8 | 4.5 | 4.0 | 3.9 | 2.8 |

Source IISS, June 1999

In early 1999, General Surayath Chulanont, the armed forces commander-in-chief, stated that Thailand would make no major military purchases 'for the next five years'.[10] Thailand's 1999 budget cut defence spending by a further 4.4% in local currency; the draft budget for 2000 envisages an increase of just 0.3%.[11]

As a result of the economic crisis, Malaysia's planned defence spending fell by at least 21% in the 1998–99 financial year.[12] In October 1998, the government started a comprehensive defence review with possible funding implications and, in March 1999, Deputy Defence Minister Abdullah Fadzil Che Wan stated that further cuts would reduce defence procurement by at least 30%.[13] Several procurement programmes, involving AEW aircraft, submarines, armed helicopters and army equipment such as armoured vehicles, artillery and air-defence missiles, were suspended, and major infrastructure projects frozen.[14] However, the long-planned acquisition of 27 patrol vessels was proceeding in early 1999, with an order for the first six signed in February.[15]

In the Philippines, the plunge in the peso's value has effectively cut by almost a third the $2bn allocated for the first five years (1996–2001) of the armed forces' 15-year, $13bn modernisation programme. The economic slowdown has also cast doubt on the longer-term viability of the plan, which had assumed 6% annual economic growth and stable exchange rates. In April 1998, the armed forces called for tenders for 24 new fighters and seven patrol vessels, to be supplied over ten years with payment stretched over 17 and 22 years respectively.[16] In July 1998, newly elected President Joseph Estrada claimed that the previous administration had left the country 'bankrupt', and that the modernisation programme would be deferred for at least a year.[17] Nevertheless, in April 1999 renewed concern over Chinese encroachment in areas of the Spratly Islands claimed by the Philippines persuaded Manila to release $150m of modernisation funding to supplement the 1999 defence budget, which had effectively been frozen at 1998 levels in US-dollar terms.[18]

In local-currency terms, Indonesia's defence budget for fiscal year 1998–99 grew by 7% over that of the previous year.[19] Although much procurement has traditionally been funded from extra-budgetary sources, the rupiah's precipitate depreciation, and the IMF's insistence that Jakarta shelve plans for military mod-ernisation, mean that the funds available for international procurement are negligible.[20] According to Indonesian Defence Minister General Wiranto, by January 1998 the country was 'not thinking about buying new military equipment'.[21] Plans to purchase Su-30 fighters and Mi-17 helicopters from Russia have been 'postponed indefinitely', as has the acquisition of five second-hand German submarines.[22] In August 1998, it was reported that pay-ments for other equipment on order, such as *Hawk* light fighters from the UK, might have to be rescheduled.[23] In February 1999, the Indonesian air force cancelled all of its contracts for locally built aircraft and helicopters.[24]

## Defence Spending in North-East Asia

With almost a third of spending allocated to procurement and research and development (R&D), South Korea remains an extremely large defence market.[25] Apart from a slight fall in 1991, the country's spending grew rapidly between the mid-1980s and 1997 under a Force Improvement Program aimed at reducing dependence on US military support. By mid-1997, however, the won's depreciation had reduced the dollar value of this expenditure. Slower-than-expected economic growth forced cuts in planned budget increases and the deferment of major procurement plans, including the F-X fighter.[26] In late 1997, an austerity programme imposed by the IMF in exchange for its assistance significantly reduced defence spending, but the continued threat posed by North Korea, combined with US pressure to maintain national defence efforts, has meant that cuts have not been as severe as in South-east Asia. Although the initial defence budget for 1998 was, in local currency, marginally higher than in 1997, and was subsequently increased by two 'defence capability enhancement projects', the won's declining value meant that overall spending was around 8% lower in dollar terms.[27] The 1999 defence budget was fixed at approximately 1998 levels, but procurement spending grew by 1–2%. In 2000, spending is expected to increase by 5.8%.[28] In early 1998, the government announced that 220 procurement programmes would be postponed or spread over longer periods, and initial funding for the development of the indigenous KTX-2 trainer was cut.[29] However, in February 1999 Seoul announced plans for major defence purchases between 2000 and 2004, including three KDX indigenous destroyers, 60 F-X fighters, attack helicopters and UAVs. Plans to buy AEW aircraft will be deferred until 2004.[30]

While Japan provides more details of its defence spending than any other country in the region, the yen's fluctuating value against the dollar during the 1990s has made it difficult to identify trends in the real value of Tokyo's expenditure. Measured in yen, spending was constant at 1% of gross domestic product (GDP), but increased gradually in absolute terms until fiscal year 1997. In dollars, expenditure rose drama- tically following the Plaza Accord of 1985, and again in 1995. From 1996, the yen's depreciation caused total spending on defence procurement to

*the first contraction in Japan's defence spending since the 1950s*

fall by over 20% in dollar terms, from $10bn in 1994 to $7.8bn in 1997.[31] In late 1998, the yen's recovery again boosted the dollar value of Japan's expenditure.

In a bid to reduce its debt burden and budget deficit, Japan cut more than $8bn from projected military expenditure under its 1996– 2000 defence build-up programme, leading in fiscal year 1998 to the first contraction in the country's defence spending since its armed forces were established in 1954.[32] Plans to acquire major equipment, such as in-flight refuelling and maritime-patrol aircraft, were re-evaluated or deferred.[33] Reduced defence spending was also used to justify the further postponement of a decision on whether to participate in the US-sponsored research programme on theatre missile defence (TMD).[34] Following North Korea's missile test over Japan in August 1998, Tokyo decided to join the programme, but substantial funding increases will not be required until the development phase begins after 2005. The 1999 procurement budget has been capped at 1998 levels.[35]

## Relatively Unscathed: China, Taiwan and Singapore

The economic crisis has not affected all states in East Asia to the same degree and, in mid-1999, China, Taiwan and Singapore appeared to have escaped relatively unscathed. Partly as a result, defence spending and procurement programmes in these countries have not suffered to the same extent as elsewhere in the region.

China's level of military spending is the most controversial in the region. After drastic cuts in the 1980s, economic boom and the increased political power of the People's Liberation Army (PLA)

**Table 3** *East Asian Economies, 1996–1999*

|  | GDP growth | | | | Change in currency value against US$ (June 1997–May 1999) |
|---|---|---|---|---|---|
|  | 1996 | 1997 | 1998 | 1999 |  |
| China | 9.6% | 8.8% | 7.8% | 8.2% | no change |
| Indonesia | 8.0 | 4.9 | -13.7 | -3.9 | -69% |
| Japan | 3.8 | -0.7 | -2.1 | -0.7 | -8.0 |
| South Korea | 7.1 | 5.5 | -5.5 | 3.7 | -26 |
| Malaysia | 8.6 | 7.8 | -7.0 | 2.0 | -34 |
| Philippines | 5.8 | 5.2 | -0.5 | 2.3 | -30 |
| Singapore | 6.9 | 8.0 | 1.5 | 2.0 | -17 |
| Taiwan | 5.7 | 6.8 | 4.8 | 4.5 | -15 |
| Thailand | 5.6 | -1.3 | -7.0 | -0.5 | -30 |

Note    GDP growth figures for 1998 are estimates; figures for 1999 are forecasts

Sources    'Prices and Trends', *Far Eastern Economic Review*, 26 June 1997, p. 74; *ibid.*, 27 May 1999, p. 64

following the Tiananmen Square massacre in 1989 have seen the official defence budget average more than 10% growth annually since 1989, reaching $11bn in 1998–99.[36] Independent estimates based on purchasing-power parity claim that actual expenditure has been considerably higher: the IISS puts it at $36.6bn in 1997.[37] Although China claims that around a third of official defence spending goes on equipment and maintenance costs, foreign military procurement and some R&D projects are widely believed to be funded by grants excluded from the defence budget.[38] Although most equipment is manufactured locally, Beijing spent an estimated $1.5bn on imports in 1996.[39] In early 1998, Defence Minister Chi Haotian claimed that Beijing was minimising defence spending in the interests of economic development.[40] However, the 12.9% increase in the official defence budget for 1998–99 indicated that modernising the military remained a priority; continued procurement at the end of the 1990s includes large numbers of Russian combat aircraft, naval vessels and surface-to-air missiles (SAMs).[41] Despite increased funding in 1998–99, the budget was overspent by 39%.[42] China's official defence budget may become increasingly stretched following the government's move to halt the PLA's commercial activities, reducing the availability of extra-budgetary funds.[43] Increasingly, the PLA is also likely to be forced to pay market prices for domestically produced equipment. China's defence budget for 1999–2000 increased by 11.5% – insufficient to compensate for the PLA's loss of extra-budgetary resources.[44]

Taiwan's military spending rose by more than 20% in real terms between 1992 and 1997. To pay for the re-equipment of the island's air force with US-built F-16C/D and French *Mirage* 2000-5 fighters, special funding allocations of some $11bn between 1993 and 2001 have supplemented the main defence budget.[45] In fiscal year 1999, the defence budget grew by 4%, although currency depreciation of 15% in 1997–99 substantially reduced purchasing power.[46] The budget for fiscal year 2000 cut defence spending by 18%. Nonetheless, procurement plans announced in 1998–99 involve some major items, notably $600m allocated to indigenous missile programmes; a $300m naval package, including three frigates from the US; $160m-worth of navigation and targeting pods for F-16 strike aircraft; and locally assembled submarines, 'stealth' fast-attack craft, and long-range radar and anti-tactical ballistic missile systems.[47]

In contrast to its South-east Asian neighbours, Singapore increased its defence budget in 1998, not only in terms of local currency and dollars, but also, according to official figures, as a proportion of GDP.[48] According to Defence Minister Tony Tan, Singapore must demonstrate that it is prepared to commit resources to defence 'in good times and bad' in order to maintain the confidence of its citizens, and that of foreign investors.[49]

## Trends

In the countries worst affected by the economic crisis – Indonesia, South Korea, Malaysia, the Philippines and Thailand – defence spending in dollars is unlikely to recover to 1997 levels in the next two to five years. Moreover, in South Korea and Thailand the crisis has brought to power governments less susceptible to military influence than their predecessors, and more likely to restrain military spending. Some ambitious procurement programmes may be deferred, but even in the worst-hit states, limited acquisitions of new equipment will continue. In Indonesia, Malaysia, the Philippines and Thailand, the emphasis is likely to be on upgrading existing equipment, particularly combat aircraft and naval vessels, involving the integration of 'more advanced subsystems and more advanced weapons'.[50]

In late 1998 and early 1999, some analysts perceived the first signs of economic recovery in East Asia.[51] But dangerous possibilities remained, including the collapse of political and social order in Indonesia, a full-blown Japanese depression, currency devaluation in China and a banking collapse in South Korea. Full regional recovery will require 'massive structural reform to the banking and corporate sectors [and] debt restructuring programmes'.[52] The longer the region's economic problems persist, the less likely it becomes that their effects will be felt simply in terms of constraints on defence spending and procurement. By damaging economic growth, developments since mid-1997 have undermined a principal foundation of East Asia's security. In the short term, the main impact will be felt internally, in terms of social stability. But longer-term implications could impinge on relations within the region, and could even upset the balance of power – encouraging states to maintain or even increase their defence spending.

## chapter 2

# International Defence Suppliers and the East Asian Market

East Asia's importance as a defence market has increased significantly during the 1990s. Following the end of the Cold War, demand for defence equipment in North America and Western Europe, and indeed in Eastern Europe and the former Soviet states, declined dramatically, forcing suppliers to look to other markets. Between 1990 and 1997, East Asia's share of global defence imports by value almost tripled, from 11.4% to 31.7%.[1] In 1988, only 10% of US arms exports went to the region. By 1997, this had increased to 25%, worth some $4bn.[2] Between 1993 and 1997, four of the world's seven largest arms-importing states were in East Asia: China, Japan, South Korea and Taiwan.[3]

## International Suppliers
### The United States
The US share of global arms exports rose from 27% in 1990 to 45% in 1997, largely as a result of the collapse of the Soviet Union's network of relationships with client states. Over the same period, the share of the Soviet Union/Russia fell from 29% to 5.4%.[4] US suppliers have consistently been the principal external sources of defence equipment for Japan, South Korea, the Philippines, Singapore, Taiwan and Thailand. US dominance in these markets has been assured by the country's strong bilateral security links which, during the Cold War, provided both political and military rationales for buying American equipment. The doctrinal and logistical dependence of regional armed forces, and concessional financing associated with the

**Table 4** *Arms Deliveries to East Asia, 1987, 1992–1997*

| (1997 US$m) | 1987 | 1992 | 1993 | 1994 | 1995 | 1996 | 1997 |
|---|---|---|---|---|---|---|---|
| China | 877 | 1,458 | 629 | 278 | 756 | 1,565 | 469 |
| Indonesia | 351 | 56 | 98 | 53 | 177 | 730 | 417 |
| Japan | 1,620 | 1,347 | 2,809 | 2,338 | 2,399 | 2,161 | 2,190 |
| North Korea | 567 | 33 | 5 | 96 | 104 | 104 | 104 |
| South Korea | 945 | 1,252 | 1,384 | 1,497 | 1,565 | 1,669 | 1,565 |
| Malaysia | 95 | 146 | 295 | 908 | 782 | 469 | 417 |
| Myanmar | 27 | 168 | 142 | 107 | 146 | 261 | 313 |
| Philippines | 95 | 157 | 66 | 96 | 94 | 104 | 156 |
| Singapore | 418 | 247 | 142 | 246 | 209 | 522 | 469 |
| Taiwan | 1,972 | 924 | 1,093 | 1,069 | 1,252 | 1,773 | 7,261 |
| Thailand | 581 | 415 | 153 | 417 | 1,147 | 730 | 600 |
| Vietnam | 2,565 | 21 | 21 | 86 | 209 | 261 | 261 |
| Total | 10,113 | 6,224 | 6,837 | 7,191 | 8,840 | 10,349 | 14,222 |

**Source** *The Military Balance 1998/99* (Oxford: Oxford University Press for the IISS, 1998), p. 272

Foreign Military Sales (FMS) scheme, have further reinforced US market dominance.

Nonetheless, throughout the 1990s non-US, particularly Western European, suppliers held a significant share of the East Asian market. East Asian states have sometimes required military equipment which has not been produced by American companies, mainly because there was no current demand for it from the US armed forces. For example, non-US, particularly European, suppliers have met East Asian needs, driven by concerns over maritime security, for diesel-electric submarines, small and medium-sized naval surface combatants and short- and medium-range maritime patrol aircraft. They have also supplied advanced training aircraft.

US restrictions on arms sales to several East Asian states have also provided opportunities for alternative suppliers. There has been considerable concern during the 1990s that Beijing has taken advantage of advanced US dual-use (civil–military) technology –

**Table 5** *Defence Contracts with East Asia, 1990–1997*

| (Current price US$bn/Market share %) | | | | | | | | | |
|---|---|---|---|---|---|---|---|---|---|
| | 1990 | 1991 | 1992 | 1993 | 1994 | 1995 | 1996 | 1997 | Total |
| US | 3.6 | 5.1 | 8.8 | 3.6 | 3.3 | 1.3 | 2.9 | 3.5 | 32.1 |
| % | 68 | 54 | 59 | 57 | 46 | 35 | 52 | 58 | 55 |
| Russia | – | – | 0.4 | 0.7 | 2.9 | 1.6 | 0.8 | 0.9 | 7.3 |
| % | – | – | 3 | 11 | 40 | 43 | 14 | 15 | 12.5 |
| France | 0.2 | 2.8 | 3.1 | 0.3 | 0.1 | 0.05 | 0.3 | 0.4 | 7.25 |
| % | 4 | 29 | 21 | 4.7 | 1.3 | 1.3 | 5.4 | 6.7 | 12.4 |
| UK | 1.1 | 0.2 | 0.9 | 1.0 | 0.4 | 0.4 | 1.0 | 0.7 | 5.7 |
| % | 21 | 2.1 | 6.1 | 16 | 5.6 | 11 | 18 | 11.7 | 9.8 |
| Italy | – | 0.9 | 0.04 | 0.05 | 0.2 | 0.2 | 0.6 | – | 1.99 |
| Germany | 0.1 | 0.2 | 0.1 | 0.6 | – | – | – | 0.3 | 1.3 |
| Netherlands | – | 0.1 | 1.5 | – | 0.08 | 0.06 | – | – | 1.74 |
| Sweden | 0.3 | 0.2 | – | 0.06 | 0.2 | 0.1 | – | 0.2 | 1.06 |
| Total | 5.3 | 9.5 | 14.8 | 6.3 | 7.2 | 3.7 | 5.6 | 6.0 | 58.4 |

**Source** UK Ministry of Defence, Defence Export Services Organisation, August
1998

particularly space technology – for military purposes.[5] Washington, however, has prohibited all sales of defence equipment to China since the 1989 Tiananmen massacre. Although the Taiwan Relations Act of 1979 allows the US to provide defensive weapons and other military equipment to Taiwan, its freedom to arm the island is constrained by the US–China communiqué of 1982, and by persistent pressure from Beijing.[6] Taiwan's purchases from the US are limited by quota to $820m-worth a year.[7] Washington's efforts to develop a 'strategic partnership' with Beijing in the late 1990s have accentuated Taiwanese concerns. Taipei has therefore diversified its sources of arms: in 1992, 60 French-built *Mirage* 2000-5 fighters were ordered at the same time as US-built F-16s, and in 1997 an arms-procurement mission was established in Western Europe.[8] However, legislation put before the US Congress in early 1999 could lead to a dramatic increase in arms sales to Taiwan. If enacted, the Taiwan Security Enhancement Act would authorise the supply of TMD systems, advanced medium-range air-to-air missiles (AMRAAMs) and *Aegis*-class destroyers.[9]

US transfers to Myanmar and Vietnam have also been ruled out for political reasons, and, since the early 1990s, the range of equipment sold to Indonesia has been restricted on human-rights grounds. Finally, Washington has restricted sales of advanced systems (for example, the AMRAAM missile and the *Longbow* attack-helicopter radar) even to significant defence partners such as Singapore and Thailand.[10] According to Joel Johnson, Vice-President for International Programs at the Aerospace Industries Association (AIA), 'the United States could claim about 70% of the market were it not for export licensing restrictions'.[11] Another AIA official, David Vadas, has claimed that US restrictions on defence sales to China, Vietnam and other East Asian states give a free hand to Russia, which 'is knocking the door down over there'.[12]

The reluctance of the US to transfer advanced defence technology, and its stringent restrictions on the export to third parties of arms produced under licence, have encouraged more industrialised states, particularly Japan and South Korea, to try to diversify their defence suppliers. In South Korea, there is a perception that US suppliers have exploited the country's alliance-related dependence on US defence equipment, and Seoul has increasingly sought European and other non-US alternatives.[13] The US share of South Korea's foreign defence procurement fell from its usual level of about 90% to 46% in 1993, as Seoul chose to buy German submarines, French SAM systems and British advanced training aircraft.[14]

*allies take US market share*

Even where US embargoes and restrictions have not pro-hibited sales, political differences and doubts over America's reliability as a supplier have worked against the country's defence companies. The view is widespread in the region, particularly in South-east Asia, that purchasing arms from the US effectively means accepting the country's political and economic values; buying equipment from other sources is equated with rejecting US 'hegemony'. This is most clearly the case in Malaysia, where the wish to project an image as a champion of non-alignment has encouraged Kuala Lumpur to choose alternative suppliers. In the

Philippines, the armed forces developed a more independent procurement system after the withdrawal of US forces in 1992.[15] In 1997–98, US congressional criticism of Indonesia's human-rights record encouraged Jakarta to look for alternative sources of fighters, transport aircraft and air-defence missiles.[16] In Singapore, the 'risks' implicit in total dependence on the US for combat aircraft may influence the air force's choice of a new fighter.[17]

## Western European Suppliers

Western European suppliers accounted for approximately 30% of the value of new East Asian international defence contracts between 1990 and 1997. The UK and France have been in the lead, between them taking more than 20% of new contracts. The key to the UK's success, particularly in South-east Asia, has been the active promotion of exports by both Conservative and Labour governments. Substantial funding has been provided under an export-credit guarantee scheme to indemnify British defence exporters to the region.[18] The Defence Export Services Organisation (DESO), part of the Ministry of Defence, has sought to expand the UK's share of East Asia's defence market, partly in order to lessen the country's reliance on exports to the Middle East.[19]

Despite occasionally serious bilateral difficulties since Mahathir Mohamad became prime minister in 1981, the UK's post-colonial relationship with Malaysia has helped defence sales. The links between the two countries include a security dimension through shared membership of the Five Power Defence Arrangements (FPDA). In 1988, Mahathir and then British Prime Minister Margaret Thatcher signed a Memorandum of Understanding (MoU), laying the basis for arms deals worth more than $2.6bn during the 1990s. Controversially, in support of the MoU, the British government provided Malaysia with almost $400m in development assistance to build the Pergau dam.[20] The UK has also maintained a 'special relationship' in defence procurement with Brunei. Britain's role as guarantor of the Sultanate's security and the presence of a British garrison there have provided the framework for major contracts. Following a bilateral protocol relating to defence procurement signed in 1989, and an MoU in 1994, British companies are expected to secure the lion's share of contracts deriving from Brunei's defence modernisation. An order in early 1998 for missile corvettes worth

$980m will probably be followed by a $300m contract for *Hawk* light combat aircraft.[21] By the late 1990s, the UK was also Indonesia's most important external source of defence equipment, with 60–70% of the market.[22] This success may partly stem from the healthy economic and – at least under the Conservatives – political relationship between the two countries, as well as from the suitability of British products such as *Hawk* aircraft and *Scorpion*-family armoured vehicles. The UK has been less successful in marketing its defence products elsewhere in South-east Asia. Partly in an attempt to remedy this, Britain entered into bilateral agreements on defence cooperation with Thailand in 1994, the Philippines in 1995 and Singapore in 1997. Although these agreements provide for joint training and exercises, and exchanges of military personnel and information, an apparent underlying aim is to promote defence sales.

North-east Asia has been considerably less important than South-east Asia to the UK's defence industry. During the 1990s, the country's largest customer has been South Korea, although sales efforts have been frustrated by aggressive US defence of its near-monopoly. British sales of lethal weapons to China have been ruled out by the European Union (EU) embargo imposed following the 1989 Tiananmen massacre. Arms sales to Taiwan are effectively banned, supposedly due to concerns over proliferation and the potential for Sino-Taiwanese conflict, though fear of diplomatic and economic reprisals by China is the real inhibiting factor. British and other European arms sales to Japan have been hampered by Tokyo's close security relations with Washington, and by Japan's need to redress its trade imbalance with the US by buying American defence equipment. Nonetheless, the UK is Japan's second most important foreign defence supplier.[23]

The UK's arms trade with East Asia has not been significantly affected under the Labour government which came to power in May 1997. Despite the concerns of non-governmental organisations (NGOs) over the trade's ethical implications, Labour's new criteria governing defence sales seem unlikely to have a profound impact, and the UK is set to maintain or even increase its share of the regional market. In early 1997, DESO identified Brunei, Indonesia and Malaysia as

*the UK is set to keep its considerable market share*

'Level 1' priority markets, in which UK sales worth at least $1,000m were thought to be achievable by 2001. South Korea, the Philippines and Thailand were seen as 'Level 2' markets, with potential sales of at least $500m. This assessment was, however, revised in the light of the region's economic crisis. Indonesia and Malaysia were demoted to Level 2, and Thailand lost this status.[24]

The French defence industry has enjoyed significant export successes in specific East Asian markets, notably Singapore and Taiwan, but has found it difficult to win more than occasional major contracts elsewhere. Singapore bought armoured vehicles, light artillery, short-range SAMs and helicopters in the early 1990s. As well as the 60 *Mirages*, Taiwan ordered three *La Fayette*-class frigates, together with associated systems and missiles, in 1992. Largely because of the delivery of 25 *Mirages* and the three frigates, defence exports to the Asia-Pacific accounted for 53% of the French total in 1997.[25] China's reaction to French arms supplies to Taiwan has been hostile and, in January 1994, Paris agreed to ban French companies from 'participating in the arming of Taiwan', although 'secondary, defensive armaments' would continue to be supplied.[26] An offer to sell submarines was withdrawn, but French defence companies continued to promote a wide range of products. Negotiations have involved additional naval equipment, further *Mirage* fighters, armoured vehicles, radar, anti-tank missiles and transport helicopters.[27] In 1995, Paris allowed the sale of *Mistral* short-range SAMs, but by early 1997 had vetoed additional contracts in a bid to avoid diplomatic conflict with Beijing ahead of President Jacques Chirac's state visit to China in May.[28] Although in January 1998 French Foreign Minister Hubert Védrine reaffirmed his country's promise not to arm Taiwan, *Apilas* anti-tank missiles were subsequently supplied, demonstrating the flexibility of the French stance.[29] French defence companies hope that the government will further relax its position; Dassault, for example, has 'actively' marketed its new *Rafale* fighter.[30]

In the 1980s, France was involved in arming China, particularly with naval systems, and some of this trade spilled over into the 1990s despite the EU's post-Tiananmen embargo. In 1989, Beijing ordered *Crotale Navale* SAM systems for its *Luda*- and *Luhu*-class frigates. These missiles were delivered in 1990, but additional units are believed to have been produced locally. Thomson-CSF *Tavitac*

**Table 6** *Major Western European Transfers of Defence Equipment, 1990–1998*

| Supplier/ recipient | Equipment type | Role | Number | Value | Order date | Delivery date |
|---|---|---|---|---|---|---|
| **Belgium** | | | | | | |
| Indonesia | F-5E/F | fighter upgrade | 12 | $40m | 1995 | 1998–99 |
| **France** | | | | | | |
| Indonesia | LG-1 Mk II | 105mm artillery | 20 | $17.5m | 1994 | 1995–96 |
| Indonesia | mission systems | for maritime patrol aircraft/helicopters | 9 | $50m+ | 1996 | n.k. |
| Indonesia | Sadral/Simbad | naval SAM | approx 240 | n.k. | 1996 | 1998 |
| South Korea | Mistral | SAM | 130+984 missiles | $186m | 1992 | 1993–96 |
| South Korea | Mistral | SAM | 1,294 missiles | $258m | 1997 | 1998–2000 |
| Singapore | AMX-10P/PAC 90 | armoured fighting vehicle | 44 | $22m | 1992 | 1991–92 |
| Singapore | Mistral | SAM | 36 | approx $20m | 1992 | 1994–95 |
| Singapore | Sadral/Simbad | naval SAM | n.k. | approx $20m | 1992 | 1994–95 |
| Taiwan | La Fayette-class | frigate | 6 | $2,800m | 1991 | 1996–98 |
| Taiwan | Mirage 2000-5 | fighter aircraft | 60 | $2,600m | 1992 | 1997–98 |
| Taiwan | MICA/Magic | air-to-air missile | 400/130 | $1,200m | 1992 | 1997–98 |
| **Germany** | | | | | | |
| ◆Indonesia | Parchim-class | corvette | 16 | $12.7m[1] | 1992 | 1993–96 |
| ◆Indonesia | Frosch-class | landing ship tank/supply ship | 14 | | 1992 | 1995 |
| ◆Indonesia | Kondor II-class | mine-countermeasures vessel | 9 | | 1992 | 1993 |
| South Korea | Type-209 | submarine | 1+8 (▲) | approx $1,500m | 1989 | 1995–2002 |
| South Korea | BO-105 | light helicopter | 12 (▲) | $110m | 1998 | 1999– |
| Malaysia | MEKO-A-100 | offshore patrol vessel | 6 (▲) | $1,280m | 1998 | 2003–06 |
| **Italy** | | | | | | |
| Malaysia | Assad-class | corvette | 4 | $500m+ | 1995 | 1997–99 |
| Thailand | G-222 | transport aircraft | 6 | $117m | 1994 | 1995–2002 |
| Thailand | Gaeta-class | mine-countermeasures vessel | 2 | $110m | 1996 | 1998–99 |

| | | | | | | |
|---|---|---|---|---|---|---|
| **Netherlands** | | | | | | |
| Singapore | Fokker 50 | maritime patrol aircraft | 5 | $20m | 1991 | 1995 |
| **Spain** | | | | | | |
| Thailand | CV-911 | aircraft carrier | 1 | $257m | 1992 | 1997 |
| ◆Thailand | AV-8S/TAV-8S | naval fighter aircraft | 9 | $90m | 1995 | 1997 |
| **Sweden** | | | | | | |
| Singapore | Bv206 | all-terrain vehicle | 300 | $60m | 1993 | 1993–94 |
| Singapore | *Landsort*-class | mine-countermeasures vessel | 4 | $200m | 1991 | 1993–95 |
| ◆Singapore | A 12-type | submarine | 4 | approx $400m | 1995/97 | 1997–2001 |
| Thailand | RBS-70 Mk II | SAM | 3+15 missiles | $4m | 1996 | 1997 |
| **UK** | | | | | | |
| Brunei | GEC-Yarrow 95m | corvette | 3 | $980m | 1995 | 2000 |
| China | *Searchwater* | maritime patrol aircraft radar | 8 | $62m | 1996 | n.k. |
| Indonesia | *Hawk* | training/ground-attack fighter | 40 | $1,030m | 1993/96 | 1996–99 |
| Indonesia | *Scorpion/Stormer* | armoured fighting vehicle | 100+ | approx $400m | 1995–97 | 1995–98 |
| South Korea | *Hawk* | training aircraft | 20 | $260m | 1991 | 1993 |
| South Korea | KDCOM | naval combat-management system | 3 | $73m | 1994 | 1998–2000 |
| South Korea | *Super Lynx* | naval helicopter | 13 | $337m | 1997 | 1999– |
| South Korea | KDCOM 2 | naval combat-management system | 3 | $75m | 1999 | 2003– |
| Malaysia | *Martello* | radar | 2 | $250m | 1990 | 1992/94 |
| Malaysia | *Starburst* | SAM | 504 | $120m | 1993 | 1994– |
| Malaysia | *Hawk* | training/ground-attack fighter | 28 | $738m | 1990 | 1994–95 |
| Malaysia | *Lekiu*-class | frigate | 2 | $600m | 1992 | 1999 |
| Philippines | *Simba* | armoured personnel carrier | 150 (142 ▲) | $46m | 1992 | 1994–96 |
| ◆Philippines | *Peacock*-class | offshore patrol vessel | 3 | approx $10m | 1996 | 1997 |
| Singapore | CET | armoured engineer vehicle | 36 | n.k. | 1993/95 | 1994–96 |

[1] For all 39 former East German ships. The cost of modernising these vessels and providing necessary infrastructural support has been estimated at $1.1bn.
▲ licence-produced; ◆ second-hand equipment

combat data systems and *Sea Tiger* surveillance radar have subsequently been fitted to *Luda* and *Luhu* frigates, as have upgraded
copies of French variable-depth sonar systems.[31]

The defence industries of other EU states are smaller than
those of the UK and France, and produce a narrower range of
equipment. They have accordingly not achieved comparable success
in the East Asian market, or indeed anywhere else. During the 1990s,
German-designed fast patrol craft, corvettes and submarines have
been produced under licence in Indonesia, Singapore and South
Korea respectively, while 39 former East German vessels were sold
to Indonesia. In 1998, a German consortium entered into a joint
venture with Malaysia's Naval Dockyard to produce patrol vessels.[32]
Germany has allowed some military exports to Taiwan, including
'offshore oil rig support ships', subsequently converted into mine-
hunters, and army bridging systems.[33] In early 1999, Germany was
also building a satellite for Taiwan, which would have significant
military applications. Germany's defence trade with China has been
discreet, but is thought to have included engines, or at least engine
technology, for *Song*-class submarines.[34] Sales to Japan have included
licences to produce FH-70 155mm artillery, and 120mm guns for
indigenously developed Type-90 tanks.[35] The coalition government
elected in October 1998 may scrutinise more closely the 'social,
environmental and developmental impact' of German arms exports
but, given the relatively uncontroversial nature of the country's
main exports, this new policy is unlikely to have a significant effect
in East Asia.[36]

Other EU states, such as Belgium, Italy, the Netherlands,
Spain and Sweden, have generally only managed sporadic and
relatively minor exports to East Asia. During the 1980s, Spain's state
aviation company, CASA, entered into a joint venture with its
Indonesian counterpart, IPTN, to develop and produce transport
aircraft. Production has continued in Indonesia in the 1990s. Spain
has also supplied Thailand with a small aircraft carrier, East Asia's
first since the defeat of Japan in 1945. Sweden's main East Asian
market has been Singapore: as well as manufacturing under licence
Swedish-designed mine-countermeasures vessels, Singapore has
bought second-hand Swedish navy submarines. In 1997, Singapore's
Defence Minister Tony Tan announced the establishment of a
bilateral 'joint research fund' to encourage collaboration in defence

R&D.[37] Sweden is believed to have helped Singapore's naval industry to design a new class of 1,000-tonne missile corvettes, which will be South-east Asia's first 'stealth' vessels.[38]

The consolidation of Europe's defence industries should help to ensure that the challenge posed to US products will be maintained, and perhaps intensified. During the 1990s, Europe's national defence industries have collaborated increasingly closely, and a wave of cross-border mergers has taken place. In December 1997, the British, French and German governments jointly urged Europe to respond to the consolidation of the US defence industry, and in July 1998 they were joined by Italy, Spain and Sweden in signing a letter of intent aimed at removing obstacles to rationalisation. In late 1998, the French government began to dismantle a serious impediment to consolidation by substantially reducing its stake in the country's defence industry.[39] While Europe's industries consolidate, however, relations between some US and European (particularly British) companies are likely to deepen, possibly leading to long-term transatlantic alliances and mergers. Eventually, this could lessen US–European rivalry in East Asian markets, and elsewhere.[40]

## Non-Western Suppliers

Non-Western defence exporters have also played a more important role in East Asia during the 1990s. Since the mid-1990s, the volume of its arms trade with China alone has made Russia once again the second-largest exporter to the region. Russia offers unit costs substantially lower than those of Western suppliers, is less inclined to restrict transfers for political reasons, has offered generous offset arrangements and has accepted barter as payment. These factors have encouraged East Asian customers to overlook shortcomings, such as Russian equipment's high life-cycle costs and inadequate supplies of spare parts.

By 1997, Russia's exports to China totalled more than \$1bn annually, accounting for approximately 40% of the total Russian arms trade.[41] Moscow's export policy has been based primarily on the need to maintain the viability and technological competitiveness of the Russian defence industry.[42] According to Valeriy Mikhaylov, the head of Russia's department for defence-related industries, proceeds from sales to China will finance the development of the 'newest types of armaments'.[43] Exports of Su-27 fighters to China have helped to fund the development of the more advanced Su-27M for Russia's air force.[44] However, Russian industry's demands for cash payments have caused tension with Beijing, which has preferred financial arrangements including a significant proportion of barter and, in some cases, for payment to be deducted from outstanding loans.[45] Apart from Su-27s, the most important Russian military exports to China during the 1990s have included *Kilo*-type submarines, *Sovremennyy*-class destroyers, S-300 SAMs and T-80U main battle tanks. China's long-term intention is to acquire the technologies to manufacture advanced weapon platforms and accompanying systems domestically, and Beijing has resisted making large purchases without first ensuring that technology is transferred. By 1997, there were more than 100 Sino-Russian defence-technology projects, mainly involving adapting Russian systems to Chinese requirements. Under a 1995 licensing agreement, China has begun to assemble between 150 and 200 Su-27s from components. Up to 70% of each Su-27 will ultimately be manufactured in China.[46] In 1998, Russia and China signed a five-year agreement on further cooperation in arms research, development and production, possibly including the transfer of Su-30 production technology and Chinese investment in Russia's next-generation fighter programme.[47]

*Russia has swept back to second place in the market*

The new Sino-Russian arms trade has caused concern, both within the region and further afield. Japan and Taiwan have objected to Russian sales of advanced defence equipment.[48] In 1995, the US warned Russia against selling SS-18 intercontinental ballistic missiles (ICBMs) to China, and, in 1997, Secretary of Defense William Cohen labelled China's acquisition of *Sovremennyy*-class ships armed with SS-N-22 missiles as a 'threat to our forces'.[49] Russia's expanding relationship with China, involving perhaps thousands of Russian scientists, engineers and technicians working in the People's Republic, has also provoked US concern, particularly over the possible transfer of technology which could assist in China's development of long-range ballistic missiles, cruise missiles and nuclear-powered submarines.[50]

Similar concerns have been voiced in Russia itself. Notwithstanding claims that the fate of the country's defence industry will depend on exports, there is no consensus within the Moscow bureaucracy that sales of arms and military technology to China on balance benefit Russia's national interests.[51] Despite much talk since the mid-1990s of a so-called 'strategic partnership' between Moscow and Beijing, many within the Russian defence and foreign-affairs community still see China as a potential threat.[52] There are also fears that China's defence industry might take advantage of licence-production arrangements to market products in competition with Russia.[53] Such worries have led to some self-restraint. In the early 1990s, for example, the Foreign Ministry blocked the sale of Tu-22M *Backfire* long-range bombers 'on the grounds that [the sale] would introduce a new and potentially destabilising offensive weapons capability into the Asia-Pacific region'.[54] Despite doubts over the wisdom of arming China, the perceived importance of Moscow's relationship with Beijing has forced Russia to adopt a 'one-China' policy with respect to arms sales.[55] Refuting rumours in late 1997 that Taiwan might purchase Su-37 fighters for use in an 'aggressor' training role, senior Russian Foreign Ministry official Leonid Moiseyev stressed that arms sales to Taiwan were 'banned'.[56]

South Korea has been Russia's second-largest East Asian export market in the 1990s. Following Seoul's agreement in 1994 to accept $209m-worth of arms in part-payment of outstanding debt, South Korea's armed forces have received Russian tanks and other armoured fighting vehicles, as well as anti-tank missiles and SAMs.[57] Additional armoured vehicles were ordered in early 1998.[58] In 1996, Seoul began seriously considering the procurement of Russian S300 long-range air-defence missile systems worth $400m, again financed mainly from Moscow's remaining debt, rather than US-made *Patriot* missiles. In an effort to dissuade Seoul from buying S300s, the US Department of Defense stressed in 1997–98 that the Russian missiles may be incompatible with South Korea's US-manufactured systems, as well as with systems deployed by US forces in the country.[59] Russia has also offered to sell submarines to Seoul.

Moscow lost its main defence market in South-east Asia, Vietnam, when Hanoi drastically cut its defence spending with the introduction of *doi moi* ('economic restructuring') in the late 1980s and early 1990s. Since the mid-1990s, however, Vietnam has bought a squadron of Su-27 fighters and two corvettes, and is building more corvettes under licence.[60] Hanoi is seeking additional arms by 2001, including more Su-27s and naval vessels, Kh-35 anti-ship missiles, and possibly submarines. It hopes to obtain at least some of this equipment in exchange for Russia's continued access to the Cam Ranh Bay naval base.[61] Elsewhere in South-east Asia, Russia has had only limited success, due to logistical complications, US pressure on potential clients, doubts over the military effectiveness of arms untested in combat, and scepticism about long-term spares supplies. However, in 1993 Malaysia bought MiG-29 fighters and air-to-air missiles. This sale injected vital funds into Russia's military-aviation industry. By buying the R-77 missile for its MiG-29s, 'Malaysia effectively underwrote its serial production'.[62] The contract also helped to fund further MiG-29 development, as well as early research on Russia's proposed equivalent of the US–UK new-generation Joint Strike Fighter.[63] In April 1999, Russia and Malaysia signed an MoU covering cooperation on military technology.[64]

Israel is East Asia's other significant non-Western supplier, with estimated sales of $2bn in 1998.[65] The country's strengths lie in areas such as 'indigenously-developed and combat-proven unmanned air vehicles (UAVs) ... electronic warfare systems, avionics suites, missile and missile defence systems and ... aircraft upgrade programmes'.[66] Many Israeli sales are clandestine, and the country's trade with the region has a low profile. Israel's main customer is China; its emphasis, unlike Russia's, is more directly on transferring military technology, know-how, sub-systems and components, rather than complete products. Israel's cooperation with China began in the early 1980s, largely in response to the declining domestic defence market. During the 1990s, technology has reportedly been supplied for:

*Israel's clandestine but crucial defence exports*

- locally built missiles, including DF-3 (CSS-2) intermediate-range and DF-15 (M-9) short-range ballistic missiles;
- PL-8H SAMs, PL-9 air-to-air missiles and an anti-tank guided weapon based on Israel's *Mapatz*;
- rearming and upgrading main battle tanks;

- the new-generation F10 fighter;
- an AEW aircraft using the *Phalcon* radar system; and
- electronic-warfare, intelligence and surveillance projects.[67]

Although still significant, Israel's defence-industrial links with China have diminished considerably since their zenith in the early 1990s. This is partly the result of US pressure, particularly since some of the Israeli technology allegedly transferred to China is of US origin, and because of the strategic implications of some transfers. But it is also due to the increasingly close Sino-Russian military relationship.[68] Exports to China have nonetheless remained important to Israel, not only economically, but also because they allegedly allow a degree of influence over Beijing's Middle East policies.[69] In September 1998, then Israeli Defence Minister Yitzhak Mordechai visited China in a bid to increase military sales.[70]

Israel's trade in military technology with China has affected its sales to Taiwan. During the 1970s and 1980s, Israel sold Taipei air-to-air missiles, small arms, mortars, multiple-rocket launchers, electronic equipment including naval fire-control and command systems and ammunition, as well as licences to produce anti-ship missiles and patrol boats. Following protests from Beijing, Israel downgraded its defence relations with Taiwan in the 1990s.[71]

Elsewhere in the region, Israel has sold UAVs, air-to-air missiles, SAMs, and air-to-surface and anti-ship missiles to Singapore, South Korea and Thailand.[72] It also exports large volumes of relatively minor equipment: the Tadiran company, for example, sells $15–20m-worth of military communications equipment to Thailand annually.[73] Israel's closest defence-industry link in South-east Asia is with Singapore, with which it has maintained a largely clandestine military relationship since the late 1960s. In the 1990s, Israel has supplied a wide variety of equipment and technology, including high-technology armour for tanks; signals-intelligence and electronic-warfare systems for corvettes and maritime patrol aircraft; and systems integration for upgraded F-5 fighters. It has also installed additional avionics, including electronic counter-measures equipment, in F-16D strike aircraft, and has assisted in developing UAVs.[74]

South Africa, a third potentially significant non-Western supplier, has tried to enter the East Asian market in the 1990s. South

Africa's combination of advanced technology, on a par with that of European industries in some areas, and its political credentials as a non-aligned developing country, may appeal to states attempting to reduce their dependence on arms suppliers from the developed world. In Malaysia, Mahathir has encouraged links with South Africa as part of his 'South–South' cooperation initiative. Kuala Lumpur has bought South African grenade launchers and electronic and signals-intelligence systems, and may buy *Rooivalk* attack helicopters.[75] South Africa has also reached an agreement on defence collaboration with South Korea.[76]

## Regional Suppliers

With few exceptions, the arms trade within East Asia has not been a significant feature of the regional market. This reflects both the relative under-development of East Asian defence industries, most of which offer few internationally credible products, and the importance of political relationships in procurement decisions. Economic rivalry and political suspicion between the region's states have generally ruled out significant arms purchases or cooperation between defence industries.

Myanmar's political isolation and Western arms embargoes have made Yangon dependent on Chinese weaponry and, in the 1990s, the country has received a wide range of equipment.[77] China has sold frigates and associated weapon systems to Thailand, continuing a close political and military relationship established during the 1980s. While suspicion of China's regional ambitions, as well as doubts over the reliability of the equipment that it supplies, make any dramatic expansion of regional sales unlikely, Beijing's relatively inexpensive exports could become more attractive to South-east Asian customers given the region's economic crisis. Other East Asian defence industries have made only relatively minor and sporadic sales in their own region. South Korea has sold armoured vehicles to Malaysia, and North Korea is reported to have supplied *Scud* missiles, mini-submarines and air-defence missiles to Vietnam in exchange for rice and other commodities.[78] Several East Asian air forces have bought Indonesian-built transport aircraft, often on a barter-trade basis. Indonesia is alleged to have exported to Taiwan German torpedoes produced under licence.[79] Singapore has supplied infantry weapons and ammunition to several regional states, including Myanmar.[80]

Only Japan's defence industry has the technological competence and potential product range to become a major exporter within the region, and further afield. It is, however, constrained by a 1967 government decision not to export arms. The majority of platforms and weapon systems produced are built under licence from US manufacturers, which would be reluctant to allow exports. Japan has nonetheless made a major contribution to the development of defence industries elsewhere in the region, particularly in South Korea, by transferring dual-use technologies.[81] It has also allowed others, Malaysia for example, to produce non-lethal equipment such as trucks under licence.[82]

## Making Procurement Decisions

Criteria such as cost, technical merit and effectiveness are usually key to procurement decisions in North America, Western Europe and Australia. In East Asia, however, these considerations often weigh less heavily than other factors. Paying commissions to key decision-makers has been a vital influence on the equipment choices of many East Asian states. In Taiwan, diversifying procurement to include non-US sources loosened central control, opening the way for senior officers to demand payments from potential suppliers. In 1995, a retired admiral was jailed for taking bribes in connection with a 1993 contract for Italian mine-countermeasures vessels; large-scale corruption may also have played a part in France's sale of frigates to Taiwan in 1991.[83] Chinese officials were also allegedly bribed in an attempt to reduce Beijing's opposition, while then French Foreign Minister Roland Dumas was alleged to have received payment to reverse the French government's initial veto of the sale.[84] By the early 1990s in South Korea, fraud and corruption were reportedly rife in air force procurement. The US Lockheed Martin company was investigated in 1995–96 regarding bribes allegedly paid in connection with the sale of F-16 fighters.[85] Corruption charges have been brought against officials involved in the purchase of *Hawker* 800 reconnaissance aircraft.[86]

*corruption and other distortions of the market*

Arms-related corruption has provoked considerable domestic political controversy in South Korea, Taiwan and Thailand. As these countries have moved closer to democratic politics in the 1990s, pressure has grown for defence procurement to become cleaner and more transparent. The economic crisis, which has focused the attention of international institutions such as the World Bank, the IMF and the Asian Development Bank (ADB) on the need to counter corruption, is likely to increase this pressure. Political change inspired by the crisis may also have an impact: in South Korea and Thailand, new governments have pressed for wholesale military reform, including more open procurement practices, following the trend set in Taiwan.[87]

Other factors exert a more overt influence on procurement decisions. During the 1990s, suppliers have increasingly needed to make special provisions, such as accepting barter payments or offering economic compensation in the form of offsets. Malaysia paid around 25% of the cost of the MiG-29s bought from Russia in 1993 in commodities, mainly palm oil; China has paid for 70–80% of its arms imports from Russia in the 1990s with consumer goods, and has accepted rice from Myanmar in exchange for artillery.[88] According to the UK's DESO:

> *Yesteryear's formula of best product, best price, and best delivery will no longer stand up to competition that offers attractive offset incentives. It is a buyer's market. Over the past decade, offset has evolved into a highly effective marketing tool that differentiates between otherwise similar products. In today's competitive marketplace, offsets can mean the difference between success and failure, sale or no sale.*[89]

'Direct' offsets involve assisting a recipient's defence industry by allowing components or platforms to be assembled locally, or through production-sharing, production under licence, technology transfer, creating authorised regional service centres, buying components from the customer and establishing joint ventures. 'Indirect' offsets involve broader development assistance in areas such as non-defence industrial and infrastructure projects, management skills and more general education. The proportion of offset can amount to the total value of a contract. Suppliers who once saw offsets as an irksome imposition have become increasingly flexible, and defence companies now routinely include bankers, traders, consultants and brokers in their offset teams.[90] For recipients, the growing import-ance of offsets has tended to widen the circle of key decision-makers beyond military officers, to include civilian politicians and senior officials.

## Developments in Arms Control

All states involved in exporting defence equipment and related technology to and within East Asia have imposed constraints on their arms trades, ranging from the extremely lax to the highly restrictive. Human-rights considerations seem not to have affected Chinese and Russian decisions on arms sales, and Moscow has sold strategically significant weapons to Beijing despite concerns that China could still pose a threat to Russia's security. Israeli guidelines on arms exports are in principle relatively strict, but in practice 'often ignored or overlooked'.[91] At the other end of the scale, Sweden and Germany have stringent controls, and Japan does not allow any arms exports at all. The US, UK and France fall between these two extremes. Pressure groups and the media, particularly in the UK, have called for stricter curbs on defence exports to developing countries in East Asia and elsewhere. It has been widely argued that, since national controls are insufficient, multilateral policies are needed, both within the EU and more widely. The most important multilateral controls have involved efforts at the European level to establish common export policies and, at the international level, the Wassenaar Arrangement.

The 33-member Wassenaar Arrangement was established in December 1995 as the successor to the Cold War's Coordinating Committee for Multinational Export Controls (COCOM). It is intended to coordinate efforts to restrict exports of sensitive or destabilising conventional arms and dual-use technologies to 'states of serious concern', or to regions of tension. The Arrangement is a voluntary, consultative forum. Although information exchanges are an essential initial step towards greater transparency, they do not necessarily lead to increased restraint, which would require a rules-based regime. In relation to East Asia, another shortcoming of the Wassenaar Arrangement is that some arms exporters – China, Israel

**Table 7** *Wassenaar Arrangement Members*

| | | |
|---|---|---|
| Argentina | Australia | Austria |
| Belgium | Bulgaria | Canada |
| Czech Republic | Denmark | Finland |
| France | Germany | Greece |
| Hungary | Ireland | Italy |
| Japan | South Korea | Luxembourg |
| Netherlands | New Zealand | Norway |
| Poland | Portugal | Romania |
| Russia | Slovakia | Spain |
| Sweden | Switzerland | Turkey |
| Ukraine | UK | US |

and Singapore – are not members. While China is a relatively minor exporter, its willingness to arm states seen as pariahs by the West undermines Western arms embargoes. For these reasons, the Arrangement as it stands is unlikely to have a major impact on exports of arms and dual-use technology to and within the region.

During the 1990s, the EU has taken several steps to regulate arms exports. In 1991, the European Council of Ministers agreed seven criteria governing arms exports; an eighth was added in 1992. The Organisation for Security and Cooperation in Europe (OSCE) agreed similar criteria in 1993. Decisions regarding the export of dual-use goods and technologies fall within the competence of EU institutions and, in 1995, member-states agreed a regulation to ensure that effective controls based on common standards across the Union were applied. However, although administrative procedures were established to iron out discrepancies between national policies, EU members were unable to reach a common interpretation of the criteria governing exports of arms and dual-use technologies. Governments have continued to pursue divergent policies; a review of the EU's dual-use regulations in 1998 found that the regime was fundamentally flawed.[92]

In July 1997, the UK's new Labour government introduced 'broad guidelines' on arms exports, intended to prevent the transfer of defence equipment which might undermine regional security, divert resources away from development programmes, or be used for internal repression. Although pressure groups have claimed that these guidelines are not rigorous enough, they have led to a more thorough screening of applications for export licences.[93] The guidelines also provided the basis for an eight-point EU Code of Conduct on Arms Transfers, which was introduced at the Union's foreign ministers' meeting in May 1998. In August, 13 non-EU European states aligned themselves with the code.[94] Under these guidelines, arms exports are not allowed to states which might use them for external aggression or internal repression, or to support terrorism. The code is, however, unlikely to affect European sales to East Asia significantly. French opposition during its formulation has weakened the code's principles by ensuring that a 'no undercutting' rule would only be applied bilaterally and confidentially. In other words, 'if a country seeking to buy arms is turned down by Britain, and then goes to France, France will inform Britain only in private that they are considering the request, rather than notifying all other EU countries'.[95] EU states will provide a detailed annual report on their arms sales to the EU Council of Ministers, but publication will be at the Council's discretion. Lack of agreement on precisely which equipment the code will cover is a further shortcoming.[96]

In the US, legislation for a code governing arms sales was introduced in the House of Representatives in 1997. Under the proposal, recipient states would need to meet criteria relating to the promotion of democracy, respect for human rights, disavowal of armed aggression, and full participation in the UN conventional arms register. The complexity of the legislative process has, however, delayed the proposal's enactment.[97] Even if the US and EU coordinated their policies on arms sales, undercutting by other exporters, such as China, Russia and Israel, would remain a problem. There have, however, been moves to develop an international code of conduct under UN auspices, similar to the EU's code and to that proposed in the US. EU governments may also seek to apply their code through the OSCE, which includes Russia.[98]

Despite the economic crisis, East Asian governments generally remain far more concerned with modernising, rather than limiting, their armed forces' capabilities. A plethora of governmental ('first track') and non-governmental ('second-track') meetings since the mid-1990s has discussed possible confidence-building measures, including greater transparency, as a first step towards regional self-restraint.[99] Tentative signs of greater openness in defence matters, such as participation in the UN conventional arms register and the issuing of so-called 'defence white papers' (usually in no way comparable to Western governments' detailed defence statements) have emerged. But the collective will to establish concrete measures such as a regional arms register is lacking.

## Trends in East Asia's Defence Market

The economic crisis is likely to constrain East Asian states' defence spending and procurement programmes for at least the next two to five years. While the impact on defence sales is hard to predict, one British industry source has forecast a 10% reduction in the sector's overall turnover by 2001.[100] Yet the crisis has not caused East Asia's defence market to collapse, and the region will remain important for US, European, Russian and other exporters. Competition between suppliers is intensifying, and the crisis will 'spur on the recent trend in the region toward demanding sophisticated offset packages, servicing agreements, follow-on technology, technology transfers, training and indoctrination. Wherever possible, [customers] will look for countertrade and instalment agreements'.[101] Israel's Tadiran company, for example, has allowed Thailand to defer payment for military communications equipment. US firm Ingalls Shipbuilding is working with a Hong Kong bank to secure finance in support of the Philippines' potential purchase of offshore patrol vessels, and French firm Dassault plans to offer 'financial incentives' to attract East Asian customers for the *Rafale* fighter.[102] Russia's state-owned defence-export agency, *Rosvooruzheniye*, plans to offer innovative finance options, emphasising barter and offsets.[103] South Korea, Singapore and Taiwan are likely to remain particularly important markets. China could become more significant as a market for a wider range of suppliers if exports are allowed to expand beyond the semi-covert transfers of European naval systems and radar, and the export of US dual-use technology. However, given Western concerns over China's often less than constructive regional security posture, the complete lifting of the embargoes on defence sales seems unlikely except in the long term.

## chapter 3

# Defence Industries in East Asia

East Asia's defence industries vary significantly in their structure, ownership, size, technological sophistication and production capabilities. North-east Asian countries are more industrialised than their South-east Asian counterparts, and so their defence industries tend to be more mature and sophisticated. Tensions are higher in North-east Asia, and the potential for conflict there is greater, contributing to a more intensive military build-up. China and Japan have large, diversified industries capable of developing major weapon systems. South Korea and Taiwan – and even North Korea – possess a broad range of capabilities, but have more limited development capacity. In South-east Asia, Singapore's defence industry is relatively sophisticated, and its capacity for semi-indigenous development is growing. Indonesia, although producing a more limited range of equipment, is particularly strong in aviation. Other South-east Asian states have only limited production facilities, but Malaysia, the Philippines and Thailand plan to expand them.

Levels of development vary within, as well as between, East Asia's national defence industries. Countries with relatively advanced capabilities in some weapon categories may have made less progress in others. South Korea's shipbuilding industry, for example, is relatively well-developed, and can produce complex warships such as destroyers. By contrast, its military-aerospace sector has not progressed beyond building equipment under licence, and R&D is limited. Taiwan has developed indigenous combat aircraft and a range of missiles, but the country's shipbuilding sector is less advanced than South Korea's.

## National Industries
### China

China has been trying to become self-sufficient in defence production since the communist victory in 1949.[1] The country's early dependence on Soviet technology and skills, and the centralised nature of its command economy, resulted in a Soviet-style defence industry, with huge state-owned corporations.[2] The breakdown in Sino-Soviet relations in 1960 isolated the People's Republic, and slowed the development of its industry. After the 1989 Tiananmen massacre, Western inputs of defence technology largely ceased. While both of these experiences reinforced China's long-term aim of self-sufficiency, achieving this still depends on outside assistance. The country's aircraft industry, for example, is weak in key areas, from basic aerodynamic design to modern radar and military turbofan engines.[3]

Given its limited access to advanced Western military know-how, China has tried to obtain dual-use technologies through civilian programmes. In 1996–97, it was alleged that China was using US supercomputers and advanced machine tools for military research and production, and telecommunications equipment to modernise military command-and-control networks. China has also been accused of exploiting space technology, supplied to assist with launching US civilian satellites, to improve the accuracy of its long-range missiles.[4] During the 1990s, the country has increasingly exploited technology from Russia, Israel and Japan. In May 1999, the US House of Representatives Select Committee issued a report – *US National Security and Military/Commercial Concerns with the People's Republic of China* – which appeared to confirm that Beijing has also made extensive use of espionage to obtain foreign technology with military applications.[5]

China's defence industry urgently needs modernising. The liberalisation of the country's economy since 1979, together with the shift in its strategic doctrine since 1992 to stress the need to conduct 'limited war under high-technology conditions', has forced the defence industry into protracted restructuring, involving downsizing, commercialisation and the reduction of central government influence.[6] However, China's inefficient industrial culture, nurtured by decades of generous state subsidies, and limited access to modern know-how present formidable obstacles.[7]

## Japan

Japan has built a sizeable defence industry in line with the concept of *kokusanka* (indigenisation), which aims to build national industrial strength and technological independence. Indigenisation is also designed to provide a basis for technology exchange, particularly with the US, and for strategic autonomy should Tokyo's crucial alliance with Washington weaken or collapse.[8] Defence production takes place within large, privately owned corporations (*keiretsu*), notably Mitsubishi and Kawasaki, and accounts for around 90% of Japan's military procurement. However, much of this local manufacturing depends on the licensed production of US systems and, as a proportion of defence spending, military R&D funding is low by the standards of the major arms-producing states. In 1998, such funding stood at 2.6% of the defence budget, compared to 13.7% in the US.[9] The country has nonetheless developed advanced capabilities in some areas, such as radar and air-to-air missiles.[10] No *keiretsu* derives more than 10.5% of its total turnover from defence sales, although aerospace divisions depend on the domestic military market for 70–80% of their business.[11]

There has traditionally been strong domestic political and industrial impetus to develop sophisticated systems autonomously, particularly since this 'allows Japanese firms to introduce locally developed dual-use technology … into military systems without sharing commercial secrets [with the US], as might be necessary in upgrading license-produced systems'.[12] There is

> *Japan's defence industry could quickly equip a much larger military*

little doubt that, if political circumstances changed drastically and sufficient resources were devoted to large-scale rearmament, Japan's defence industry could quickly equip much larger armed forces.[13] Washington has, however, intervened to ensure that Tokyo remains dependent on US industry, partly to redress the massive bilateral trade imbalance, and partly because of fears over the strategic and commercial implications of an independent Japanese arms industry.[14] In 1987, US pressure forced Japan to abandon plans to develop an indigenous fighter aircraft; instead, Tokyo agreed to co-develop what amounted to an advanced variant of the US F-16C/D. In 1990, US companies were guaranteed 40% of the work on this 'F-2' programme, as well as a share in the rights to new technologies derived from the project. The US has insisted on what it calls 'fair exchange' of expertise, particularly access to Japanese dual-use technologies.[15]

During the 1990s, Japanese contractors have increasingly seen collaboration with European and US suppliers as potentially compensating for the decline in procurement budgets, which has left the local defence industry operating at just 30–50% of capacity. The ban on most defence exports makes it difficult to maximise the benefits of collaboration, encouraging Japanese industry to press the government to review the policy.[16] In the meantime, R&D investment has to be amortised across short production runs. This means that unit costs for 'indigenous' systems are high: each F-2, for example, is more than three times more expensive than a comparable US-built F-16.[17]

## South Korea

The development of South Korea's defence industry has been under way since the early 1970s, driven by concern over the volatile regime in the North, and by the long-term implications of reductions in US forces on the Peninsula. Although at first the US was actively supportive, the free transfer of technology ended in the early 1980s. This encouraged Seoul to expand its defence industry aggressively, in a bid to become more self-sufficient in aerospace, electronics and shipbuilding, and in the production of armoured vehicles and small arms.[18] Defence R&D spending almost quadrupled in real terms between 1987 and 1996.[19]

Most defence production takes place in large private corporate groups (*chaebol*) such as Daewoo, Hyundai and Samsung, but accounts for only a small percentage of their total output. The *chaebol* have used their cash-rich civilian divisions to subsidise expensive and sometimes unprofitable defence R&D programmes. Samsung used profits from its semiconductor business to support attempts to become a serious player in military aerospace, initially through the KTX-1 training-aircraft project and the KTX-2 advanced trainer.[20] Although the US has traditionally been South Korea's main source of technology, Seoul's drive to diversify its procurement has meant that European companies have helped to develop its defence industry. German engines have been incorporated into armoured vehicles, the French *Crotale* NG missile has been used as the basis for the indigenous *Chon-ma* air-defence system, and the Swiss firm Pilatus was involved in the design of the KTX-1.

Despite its superficial success, South Korea's defence industry has run into problems. During the 1990s, low rates of production have led to significant financial losses, and the industry still depends heavily on foreign components, raw materials and technology.[21] Efforts to develop an indigenous helicopter, for example, have failed, despite over 20 years' experience of producing US designs under licence.[22] While the Ministry of National Defence has claimed that 79% of its procurement by value is produced locally, the US government estimates that only 20% can accurately be described as indigenous.[23]

## Taiwan

Taiwan's efforts to create a self-sufficient defence industry are driven primarily by its adversarial relationship with China and its relative international isolation. Since the 1970s, Taipei has encouraged defence industrialisation through the Chung Shan Institute of Science and Technology (CSIST), which has focused on military aviation, missiles and rockets, electronic systems and chemical products such as propellants.[24] Taiwan's efforts have been described as 'a sort of technology laundering scheme', and many of its supposedly indigenous products as 'licensed copies of foreign systems or assemblages of imported components'.[25] The US has been a major source of technology for Taiwan's nascent defence industry. When the formal US–Taiwan security link was severed in 1979, US policy on supplying arms to Taipei became hostage to Washington's relations with Beijing, but 'there was little restriction on technical assistance'.[26] In the 1970s and 1980s, the CSIST's Aero Industry Development Centre (AIDC) built more than 300 F-5 fighters under licence from Northrop, providing 'invaluable experience in modern fast-jet manufacturing methods and techniques, and forging a useful link between AIDC, Northrop and … other US aerospace firms'.[27] Subsequently, Northrop and the AIDC jointly developed Taiwan's indigenous jet trainer, the AT-3.[28] The AIDC received considerable help from the US General Dynamics company when developing the Indigenous Defence Fighter (IDF) during the 1980s.[29]

Taiwan's success in securing substantial arms supplies from the US and France during the 1990s – notably the F-16s and *Mirage 2000s* – has affected the local defence industry in two main ways. First, the rationale for indigenous programmes has been undermined. By the late 1990s, around half of the procurement budget was being spent on imported systems; the IDF's planned production run, for example, was halved.[30] Second, technology inputs may widen. As a result of its 1992 order for *Mirages*, Taiwan concluded a $700m offset agreement with Dassault in 1996, which will 'transfer technology to AIDC'.[31]

## South-East Asia

The development of defence industries in South-east Asia has generally been driven less by strategic influences, and more by economic development plans, prestige factors and, in some cases, the ambitions of political leaders. In Malaysia, for example, cultivating a local defence industry is part of Mahathir's 'Vision 2020' plan to transform the country into a developed nation by 2020. In Indonesia, former President Suharto enthusiastically supported defence-related industrial programmes led by B. J. Habibie, the one-time Minister for Research and Technology who replaced Suharto as national leader in May 1998. Under Habibie, ten state-funded civil–military 'strategic industries', including aerospace, shipbuilding and electronics, have been developed since the 1970s. These industries, supported by privileged access to extra-budgetary resources and orders from a 'captive market' in the armed forces, were to be the basis for modernising Indonesia's economy.[32] Habibie's plans have, however, provoked controversy throughout the 1990s, including opposition from the politically powerful military. Senior officers have doubted the reliability of domestically produced equipment, often preferring 'off the shelf' purchases from Western suppliers.[33]

Singapore's substantial, relatively sophisticated and largely state-owned defence industry is the most diverse and capable in South-east Asia. In contrast to Indonesia and Malaysia, it was developed primarily for strategic reasons stemming from the country's vulnerability. Singapore is small, and sandwiched between two much larger and potentially threatening neighbours. Although mainly supplying the needs of its own armed forces, the defence industry is increasingly successful in niche markets abroad. Its strengths lie in upgrading combat aircraft and army equipment, and in designing, developing and producing small and medium-sized naval vessels, artillery and armoured vehicles. Singapore's defence industry, which is supported by an effective Defence Science Organisation, has drawn technology from a variety of foreign sources, notably Israel and Sweden.

## Influences on East Asia's Defence Industries
### Political, Strategic and Economic Factors
Real or perceived external security threats as well as arms embargoes are important in encouraging governments to promote domestic defence production. Asserting national sovereignty and enhancing national prestige have also been important influences. Most East Asian governments view indigenous arms production as an indispensable attribute of a modern, industrialised sovereign state. Establishing or developing defence industries has also often been seen as a way of boosting economic development more generally.[34] Defence production can be intended to increase employment opportunities, realise economies of scale in supplier industries, and create links with the rest of the economy by encouraging a supplier chain, thereby stimulating demand in industries with surplus capacity.[35] Acquiring defence technology and industrial skills may also be expected to benefit the wider economy.

These economic advantages may not, however, be so clear-cut. Creating new links between economic sectors depends on the maturity of the industrial and skills base. For Japan and South Korea, the technological and production capabilities of their iron, steel and electronics industries, for example, *the limited value of defence industries for the civil economy* are compatible with the defence sector. Where such capacity does not exist, links between defence-related aerospace, electronics and shipbuilding industries and other sectors are unlikely to be made. Instead, a gap may develop between a relatively high-technology defence sector and the rest of the economy. In Indonesia, for example, the aviation and defence industry forms a high-technology enclave alongside relatively poorly developed civilian industries.[36]

Links between the two have been minimal. In other countries in the region, including South Korea, the 'multiplier effects' of the defence industry on the civilian economy have also been disappointing. Nonetheless, no East Asian government is likely to view its defence industry as dispensable, even in the difficult economic circumstances after July 1997.

## Offsets and Technology Transfer

The transfer of technology is a crucial influence on the development of East Asia's defence industries. Since the 1950s, licence-building has been an important way of acquiring design know-how and production technology, particularly for China, Japan, South Korea and Taiwan. From the early 1970s, surplus capacity and over-production among Western arms producers, particularly in the US, encouraged them to transfer basic military-related technology and production facilities to the region's more advanced countries. The Nixon Doctrine of 1969, which reduced direct US security commitments in the region but promised continued aid and assistance to America's allies, reinforced this trend. During the 1970s, South Korea received 881 'technical data packages' from the US, 124 of which were used to establish the country's defence industry.[37]

For both political and economic reasons, during this early phase the US firmly controlled design, production and distribution. Technology transfer took the form of licensed production of components and parts and, in some cases, assembling weapon platforms. These transfers were used to induce compliance with Washington's foreign-policy goals. When allies have come close to producing advanced weapons thought to be destabilising, the US has tried to block further development by promising concessions, or by threatening sanctions, such as ending military assistance. South Korea received conventional arms and technology in exchange for freezing its NHK-A ballistic-missile programme in 1990, while Taiwan has been particularly vulnerable to US sanctions.[38]

Since the 1980s, offsets have often included specified requirements for technology transfer. Technology may also be transferred through espionage, or through a process known by Western defence companies as 'techno-suck', whereby states persuade foreign firms seeking contracts to divulge useful data. Technology transfer includes:

- blueprints and technical data for producing complete weapon systems;
- components, machine tools and manufacturing know-how;
- training and technical assistance for new production processes; and
- complete factories or production lines.

Transactions may be one-way, where the supplier provides production technology, or collaborative ventures producing systems or components for both countries, and sometimes for export to third parties.

In general, only the more industrialised East Asian states – Japan, South Korea, Singapore and Taiwan – have sufficient technological capacity for co-production or production under licence. South Korea's 1992 agreement to buy 120 F-16s from the US involved assembly from parts or licensed production by Samsung of most of the aircraft under the Korean Fighter Program, as well as substantial technical support from Lockheed Martin for design and development work on the indigenous KTX-2 trainer.[39] Lockheed Martin, as part of its offset obligation for the sale of 150 F-16s to Taiwan, has sought Taiwanese tenders for repair contracts for more than 500 aircraft components. Taiwan sees the offset programme as an opportunity to develop a regional aircraft maintenance centre and to obtain work on other aircraft being developed by Lockheed Martin.[40] All future Taiwanese purchases of advanced weapons will be conditional on offsets worth at least 30% of the contract value.[41] (Other East Asian states demand offsets of even larger proportions; they totalled some 60% of the value of Malaysia's 1990 order for British *Hawk* aircraft, for example.) While Japan has no formal offset policy, all of its major foreign defence procurement involves licence-production arrangements. Singapore claims to have no formal requirements for offsets, but often obliges major suppliers to enter into 'Industrial Cooperation Programmes' designed to benefit its defence sector by transferring technology.[42] In return for the contract to modernise Singapore's F-5 fighters, Israeli Aircraft Industries has included Singapore Technologies Aerospace (ST Aero) in consortia tendering for similar work in third countries.

Less-developed states have tried to boost their defence industries in similar ways. In Indonesia, the licensed manufacture of the Spanish CASA 212 light transport aircraft was followed by the joint development and production of the larger CN-235, providing the basis for a dual civil–military aerospace industry which, by the mid-1990s, was trying to develop larger commercial aircraft independently. However, as technology becomes more complex and sophisticated, its absorption by local industry requires ever-greater scientific and engineering knowledge. As a result, Indonesia, Malaysia, the Philippines and Thailand have often opted for indirect offsets, typically involving skills training and infrastructure development. In Malaysia, 'defence related offsets are now viewed in terms of Malaysia's broader industrialisation programme'.[43] British Aerospace sponsors the training of Indonesian aerospace engineers in the UK as part of the offset arrangements related to the purchase of *Hawks*.[44] However, buy-backs, in which the supplier purchases components produced in the recipient country, are also widespread. Indonesia's IPTN, for example, makes parts for F-16s. Malaysia's SME builds wing pylons for *Hawks*, and Daewoo of South Korea provides components for Lockheed P-3 patrol aircraft and Westland *Lynx* helicopters.

Buy-backs and some other forms of offset can damage supplier industries. For instance, a Japanese firm received technical and manufacturing assistance from McDonnell Douglas to produce flight-control components for F-15s. The Japanese firm then won the contract to provide similar components for Boeing 777 airliners, defeating a US competitor.[45] The US government has become increasingly sensitive to the potential competitive implications of technology transfers, particularly for suppliers of sub-systems and components.[46] Although the US is likely to remain East Asia's primary source of military technology, the US Congress has generally refused to pass on leading-edge technologies such as advanced materials, software and avionics. Washington has imposed a limit of 30% of a contract's value on offset deals with South Korea.[47] Supplier countries in Western Europe are also wary about the long-term implications of offsets, as is Russia.

Given the costs of keeping up with the fast pace of technological innovation, many East Asian arms producers have turned instead to add-on engineering, add-up engineering and retrofitting. Add-on engineering involves importing a weapon system, which is produced under licence, studied and reverse-engineered, then adapted to domestic requirements. Taiwan has used this technique to develop the *Hsiung Feng* anti-ship missile from Israel's *Gabriel*, and North Korea has produced an array of ballistic missiles based on Soviet systems, such as the *Frog*-7 and *Scud*-B.[48] Add-up engineering integrates components and technologies from various sources into a new weapon system: Taiwan's development of the air-launched *Hsiung Feng* 2 missile, Japan's F-2 programme, Taiwan's IDF and South Korea's K-1A1 main battle tank were all developed in this way.[49] Retrofitting or upgrading integrates new sub-systems into an existing platform to improve its operational capabilities and lengthen its service life. Singapore's upgrading of its F-5E/F fighters by fitting more advanced avionics, radar and other systems is a typical example.[50]

## Changes in East Asia's Defence Industries

During the 1990s, several factors have changed the structure, ownership patterns and levels of development of East Asia's defence industries. These include the 'civilianisation' of production, and restructuring, typified by growing commercialisation, privatisation and closer international collaboration. The economic crisis has accelerated this process.

### The Role of Civilian Industry

Defence equipment increasingly relies on technology derived from civilian industries. As global defence markets shrink and civilian ones expand, the cost of defence R&D is rising, and the ability to absorb civilian technology, adapt it to military ends and integrate it into defence systems is increasingly important. Industrial 'spin-on' from civilian to military applications could become particularly significant in East Asia because of the prowess of some regional states' civilian information-technology sectors.

'Spin-on' is most apparent in Japan. The country has East Asia's most sophisticated industrial base, which manufactures a large volume and variety of dual-use technologies, parts and components. Its industrial structure, based on large, horizontally ordered conglo-merates, encourages the diffusion of technology, and Japan's political leaders do not strictly separate industrial, technological and

*the new importance of 'spin-on' technology*

national-security concerns.[51] A widening range of commercially developed technologies – electronics, composite materials and ceramic components, for example – is being integrated into advanced military systems.[52] Japan's 1997 defence white paper recognised the significance of civilian high technology for military systems such as electronics, aircraft, guided weapons, firearms, ammunition, vehicles and underwater measurement.[53] Under procurement reforms introduced in 1997, 'about half of the 18,000 military standards' in use will be 'simplified, if not eliminated, by 2000' to make more effective use of civilian technologies.[54]

Other East Asian states, including China, South Korea, Singapore and Taiwan, are also trying to exploit dual-use technologies. South Korea plans to triple its budget for government-led research on dual-use technologies in 1999–2002.[55] In China, senior defence-industry and military leaders have emphasised the importance of applying civilian technology.[56] In practice, however, exploiting this technology has proved difficult: Chinese defence and R&D personnel reportedly 'often disdain civilian technology that might otherwise be "spun on"'.[57] The most important civilian inputs into China's defence industry have been Western management techniques and production machinery. In Taiwan, the defence establishment has also tried to enhance 'spin-on', although opposition politician Parris Chang has claimed that the island's high-technology industry could be better used.[58] In Singapore, the government's Defence Science Organisation has implemented programmes aimed at harnessing dual-use communications and computing technology to military purposes, while the country's defence industry is concentrating on using 'cost-effective' commercial off-the-shelf technologies.[59]

Japan and South Korea increasingly provide critical subsystems and components, such as silicon chips and liquid-crystal displays, for US weapon systems, causing concern in the Pentagon over the security of supplies.[60] Observers have argued that the traditional pattern of technology dependency could be reversed, with the West becoming reliant on East Asia for key items of military equipment.[61] By 1991, Japan had matched or exceeded NATO countries in nine out of the 11 generic technologies identified by the US Department of Defense as key for future defence systems.[62] Japan's technological advances have encouraged US and Japanese manufacturers to set up joint development programmes covering, for example, the use of ceramic technologies in vehicle engines, and advanced steel for warships and armoured vehicles.

The strengths of East Asian industries in key dual-use technologies could have wider implications for the type of defence equipment which they might produce and export in the future. In 1996, aerospace and defence electronics analyst Len Zuga argued that the growing capabilities of Japan, South Korea, Singapore, Taiwan and even Malaysia were leading to a situation where, in areas such as electronic warfare, 'these nations will provide credible competition in the marketplace in much less time than US manufacturers believe possible'.[63] The extent to which civilian high technology has boosted East Asia's defence industries may, however, be overstated. Australian academic Paul Dibb has pointed out that, although the region's 'economic, technological and educational advances' are 'relevant to improving military capabilities', these 'highly advanced skills are in short supply'.[64] In China, 'there is a long-standing tradition of separation of the commercial and military sectors', and bureaucratic and ideological impediments have stifled high-quality R&D. As a result, China's military manufacturers have had to 'rely largely on reverse engineering rather than technological innovation'.[65] Even in Japan, 'there has been insufficient progress in developing complex semiconductors, such as microprocessors, advanced software and computing technology'.[66] Analyst Michael Green has highlighted the lack of systems-integration skills, 'the ultimate goal in terms of military autonomy', as a

*few East Asian states can keep up with the pace of innovation in the West*

critical Japanese shortcoming.[67] Relatively slow advances in areas such as 'fire-control systems, missile guidance, and flight- and engine-control systems' underline this deficiency.[68] Similarly, while South Korea produces major warships, it relies on foreign sources for vital combat-management and fire-control systems.[69] These weaknesses are even more serious elsewhere in East Asia, and particularly affect attempts to integrate combat systems for aircraft and warships. Problems encountered in Singapore's programme to outfit its F-5 fighters with new radar, and in Indonesia's efforts to develop a maritime patrol version of the CN-235, are typical.[70] Dibb concludes that 'the capacity to modify and adapt complex military systems (especially source codes) will be limited to a very few countries in Asia – Australia, Japan and Singapore – and even they will depend heavily on collaboration with US and European companies'.[71]

## Diversification

Another strategy has been to diversify into civilian production. Since the mid-1990s, Japanese *keiretsu* divisions which have traditionally focused on defence production have been trying to reduce their reliance on the Japan Defense Agency (JDA) for business.[72] In South Korea, major aerospace manufacturers have tried to become involved in international civil-aircraft projects, and to secure additional civilian subcontracting work.[73] According to the Chinese government, civilian goods accounted for 80% of the value of the defence industry's output by 1994, compared with 8% in 1979.[74] China's aviation industry, which has traditionally relied on domestic defence procurement, is increasingly supplying components for Western manufacturers of civil airliners.[75]

The region's smaller defence industries are moving in the same direction. By the mid-1990s, the Singapore Technologies Group had reduced defence production to 62% of its total business by diversifying into civilian activities such as telecommunications, electronics, computers, aerospace, commercial logistics and precision engineering.[76] ST Aero, which aims to reduce its defence activities to 30%, has developed and produced the EC-120 light helicopter with Chinese and French partners.[77] By 2003, Taiwan's AIDC intends to derive 40% of its revenue (compared with 20% in 1997) from civilian activities, such as producing tail sections for Boeing 717 airliners and cockpits for Sikorsky S-92 helicopters.[78] This trend has been reflected in more indirect, non-defence offsets. In return for its *Mirage* 2000 deal with Taiwan, for example, Dassault has contracted the AIDC to produce components for *Falcon* civilian transport aircraft.[79]

## Restructuring and Changing Ownership Patterns

In most East Asian countries, the state has traditionally played a major role in establishing, organising and controlling defence industries. However, changing political and economic conditions in the 1990s, particularly the pressure to commercialise, privatise and remove government subsidies, are affecting patterns of ownership and control, and the role of the private sector is increasing. The economic crisis has intensified these pressures since 1997.

In South Korea, government pressure for corporate down-sizing and restructuring is likely to end the heavy subsidies for the defence industry from the more profitable commercial divisions of the *chaebol*.[80] Seoul has also decided that the number of major defence contractors should be reduced from 19 to 12.[81] In September 1998, Daewoo, Hyundai and Samsung agreed in principle to merge their aerospace businesses into an independent consortium, Korean Aerospace Industries, in June 1999.[82] The government has also decided to allow foreign companies to invest in, take over or merge with local defence and aerospace firms.[83] European and US manu-facturers have been offered a 50% stake in Korean Aerospace.[84] In Indonesia, IMF pressure had by early 1998 forced the government to withdraw financial support for IPTN (which will have to cut its work-force by a third by 2001) and other strategic industries.[85] Although this may not prevent state funds from reaching these industries indirectly, it is likely to hamper the sector's development plans. In Malaysia, which has not sought IMF help, there are indications that the government will assist companies deemed of 'strategic interest', such as those in the automotive, aerospace and shipbuilding sectors.[86] Nevertheless, Airod and three other aero-space firms will be forced to merge in order to reduce the government's costs and increase the sector's competitiveness.[87] In the early 1990s, several Singapore Technologies subsidiaries were publicly listed on the stock market.[88] Taiwan's AIDC is slated for partial privatisation in 1999, although 30% will remain in state hands.[89] The Thai government sees joint ventures between public and private sectors as a way to increase efficiency and obtain new technologies.[90]

The Chinese government recognises that restructuring is necessary to deal with the many shortcomings of its defence sector, notably 'excessive industrial over-capacity, chronic inefficiency, capital shortages and low technological standards'.[91] The industry will nonetheless remain state-owned. In April 1998, the defence industry was reorganised, and the military and civilian components of the Commission for Science, Technology and Industry for National Defence (COSTIND) were separated. The military portion (the General Equipment Department (GED)) will be responsible for procurement policy, including foreign purchasing, while the new civilian-controlled COSTIND will manage R&D, defence production, the conversion of defence industries to civilian production, and arms exports.[92] By around 2005, only 200–300 of the several thousand existing Chinese defence enterprises are intended to be producing defence equipment. A small number of new commercialised state corporations are supposed to control surviving enterprises in the nuclear, aviation, space, ordnance and shipbuilding sectors.

## International Links

International cooperation has played a vital role in the development of East Asia's defence industries since the 1960s. During the 1980s and 1990s, however, there has been a more pronounced shift away from traditional, single-country patterns, towards strengthening international links in R&D, production and marketing.[93] Co-production, joint ventures and co-development have increased, albeit at different speeds in different sectors. Defence electronics and aerospace, for example, are considerably more 'internationalised' than shipbuilding or mechanical engineering, which depend less on advanced foreign technology. National policy may favour or discourage international links, depending on whether import substitution or more outward-oriented strategies are pursued. China's defence industry has established strong ties with its counterparts in Russia and Israel, and has allowed foreign investment in its civil aerospace sector; in July 1997, Beijing announced that it would permit foreign investment in its defence industry.[94] Russia's relative weakness in information technology and communications gives Beijing a particular interest in encouraging Japanese and Western participation in upgrading its defence-electronics industry.[95]

While developing more international links may be increasingly necessary, achieving this is not always straightforward. Japan's blending of technological, industrial and security policies (often summed up as 'techno-nationalism'), and its ban on arms exports have made it difficult for the country's defence industry to participate in international programmes. Despite its prowess in many areas of technology, Japan's industry needs considerably deeper international links if it is to nurture the design and systems-integration skills necessary to develop and produce high-technology military systems efficiently. In August 1998, Mitsubishi Electric announced a potentially significant alliance with Lockheed Martin to develop missile-guidance systems, weapon controls, electronic-warfare systems and air and naval radar, and to market this equipment to the JDA.[96] Political and technical setbacks have plagued some of South Korea's collaborative projects, such as the Type 88 tank and the more advanced K-1A1, which is based on the US M-1 *Abrams*. The KTX-2 trainer has also been affected.[97] Collaboration is nonetheless the only practicable way forward. Incipient South Korean projects may include Russian assistance in developing submarines and a medium-range SAM.[98] Political considerations also hamper international collaboration in Taiwan. A joint venture between the AIDC and Northrop Grumman to develop an upgrade programme for ageing F-5E/F fighters collapsed in 1998, allegedly partly because of US government reluctance to allow Taiwan to export F-5s retrofitted with AGP-66 radar systems, or to release relevant software technology.[99] The AIDC will instead cooperate with Singapore's ST Aero.[100] Singapore's defence industry has joined the US–UK Joint Strike Fighter programme as an 'informed participant', and is involved in advanced naval research with Sweden.[101]

In contrast to the ever-denser web of links between defence companies in Western Europe, collaboration between East Asian industries has not progressed far. In 1995, Malaysia and Singapore signed a memorandum on cooperation, and, in the same year, Habibie called for the integration of the defence industries of Indonesia, Australia and Japan.[102] But political suspicions, lack of trust in defence and security matters between regional states, and competitive industrial strategies are likely to preclude substantial collaboration for the foreseeable future.

In the expansionist climate fostered by sustained economic growth before the 1997 crisis, East Asian companies and governments had begun to look into buying stakes in Western defence-related enterprises. In 1996–97, both the Malaysian government and South Korea's Samsung showed interest in taking major shareholdings in the ailing Fokker company, a Dutch manufacturer of civilian and military transport aircraft. For Malaysia, the tentative move indicated 'frustration after several joint-venture partners ... delayed transferring much-needed technologies'.[103] In 1997,

Malaysia's Business Focus Group, the majority shareholder in Naval Dockyard, expressed interest in acquiring stakes in leading Australian defence companies, such as Australian Defence Industries and Australian Submarine Corporation, on their privatisation.[104] However, the economic crisis will largely rule out further developments along these lines, at least any involving South Korean and Malaysian firms.

Limited domestic demand has encouraged East Asian producers to enter the international arms market, both in the region and beyond. China and North Korea have exported substantial quantities of relatively low-technology, but strategically significant, ballistic missiles, particularly to the Middle East and Pakistan. Singapore's defence industry has been successful in the growing retrofitting market, exporting upgrade programmes for F-5 fighters to Venezuela and, in conjunction with Israeli companies, to Turkey.[105] Malaysia's Airod is marketing its aircraft-overhaul services beyond South-east Asia.[106] Despite these developments, the value of East Asian defence exports is almost negligible as a proportion of the global arms trade. China, East Asia's most important exporter, saw its share of the global market fall from a peak of 3.3% in 1992 to 2.2% in 1997.[107] Declining demand in the global market limits Asian exports, while the need for permission to export to third parties constrains industries dependent on producing and developing US systems under licence.

## The Economic Crisis and the Future of East Asia's Defence Industries

The economic crisis may accentuate the long-standing inclination of some East Asian governments to become more self-sufficient in defence production. In January 1998, South Korea's Ministry of National Defence announced plans to develop indigenous anti-ship missiles, self-propelled artillery and SAMs, as well as buying locally produced coastal-surveillance radar, radios and ammunition.[108] In May 1999, Prime Minister Kim Jong Pil revealed that Samsung Aerospace Industries would produce an extra 20 F-16C/D fighters, costing $663m, in order to provide work for the local aviation industry. Funding would come from outside the defence budget.[109] Malaysian Defence Minister Syed Hamid Albar has emphasised the need to reduce 'dependence on foreign equipment' in the armed forces, and the local production of relatively unsophisticated equipment such as military vehicles is likely to increase.[110] However, given stagnant or declining defence spending, a substantial shift towards greater domestic production, let alone design and development, is unlikely. Sales by South Korea's defence industry slumped by 45% in 1998, illustrating the depth of the problem in parts of the region.[111]

While the defence industries of most East Asian states will survive, the crisis has forced the pace of restructuring, and has made international links more important in the worst-affected countries. If prolonged, it may sound the death-knell for some major planned projects in Japan, South Korea and Taiwan. But collaborative ventures with US and European companies, including joint development projects, co-production and sub-contracting, remain likely. Where East Asian governments can find the resources to make major purchases of foreign equipment, they will continue to extract valuable offsets. High-technology civilian industries in Japan, South Korea and, possibly, Singapore and Taiwan will probably allow these countries to play more important roles as joint-venture partners, and as suppliers of sub-systems and components in an increasingly globalised defence industry.

*the economic crisis has forced the pace of reform in defence industries*

## chapter 4

# Changing Military Capabilities and the Regional Balance

New, more sophisticated conventional weapon systems have proliferated throughout East Asia during the 1990s. However, acquiring hardware does not automatically mean better military capabilities. Qualitative factors – adequate numbers of well-trained, motivated personnel, efficient logistics, comprehensive doctrine, effective operational cooperation between branches of the armed forces, and high readiness levels – are critical in distinguishing those armed forces which are developing real capabilities, from those which are merely purchasing expensive equipment with little genuine military utility.

## The RMA and East Asian Armed Forces

To some extent, relevant doctrine is passed on with military equipment through training arrangements with suppliers, and industrial offsets may increase recipients' logistical and maintenance capabilities. But the impact of the technological and doctrinal developments known as the RMA must also be taken into account.[1] To benefit from the RMA, armed forces must undergo fundamental doctrinal, logistical and organisational changes, as well as acquiring relevant equipment.

During the 1990s, the growing importance of maritime security issues in East Asia means that the acquisition of air and naval systems has been particularly striking. But some of the most significant procurement has involved 'invisible' systems. Although they have received relatively little publicity, these systems are crucial force multipliers, and could help regional armed forces to participate in the RMA. They include:

- advanced command, control and communications systems, sometimes using satellites;
- technical intelligence systems, including signals intelligence and high-resolution satellite imaging;
- electronic-warfare systems;
- advanced radar and sonar systems; and
- precision-guided munitions.

Even with the benefit of equipment such as this, however, the shortcomings of most regional armed forces make absorbing many aspects of the RMA difficult. Too little attention has been paid to integrated logistic support or systems integration, and joint-force doctrine and organisation are underdeveloped. Shortcomings in national defence industries and defence science organisations may also limit RMA capabilities. In some East Asian states, notably China, political factors may stifle the innovative thinking needed in order to develop and integrate advanced information and communications systems.[2] Finally, even if East Asian defence spending had continued to grow rapidly, most states would only have been able to afford thoroughgoing adoption of the RMA in the long term.

RMA-based armed forces are not necessarily panaceas for East Asia, particularly South-east Asia where low-intensity security problems prevail. Nonetheless, those states able to deploy even limited RMA-based capabilities may dramatically improve their capacity to detect, target and destroy enemy aircraft, ships and armoured vehicles – and will probably gain distinct military advantages over neighbours lacking similar capabilities. The RMA, or elements of it, is likely to deepen existing military disparities, both within the region, and between East Asia and the US.

## National Military Capabilities

The scale and variety of its programme of military modernisation make China the region's most significant power. During the 1990s, China has tried to transform cumbersome army-dominated forces designed to wage a territorial 'People's War' into a streamlined, hard-hitting modern military, capable of winning a limited, high-technology war on the country's periphery. For Beijing, such a conflict is most likely to occur in relation to Taiwan, or over the disputed claims in the South China Sea. The most important aspects of this modernisation process are:

- the personnel strength of the armed forces will be reduced from three million to 2.5m between 1997 and 2000, and the proportion of professional soldiers increased to 35%;
- the army is developing rapid-reaction 'fist' divisions structured for offensive operations;
- the air force is re-equipping with modern combat aircraft, such as the Russian-supplied Su-27 and the indigenous F-10, with AEW aircraft in prospect; and
- the navy is acquiring modern surface combatants, submarines and amphibious ships.[3]

While most of China's military equipment will still be produced domestically, arms and technology from Russia, Israel and the West are vital to its modernisation programme.

Although China's navy could pose a challenge to US forces, potentially in the Taiwan Straits, there is no evidence that Beijing's ability to project naval power to more distant waters, such as the South China Sea, has dramatically increased. Most of the country's major warships are lacking in air-defence and anti-submarine capabilities, and only a handful have modern combat data systems. The navy's amphibious transport capacity is limited. Chinese air force and naval air force equipment is largely obsolescent, and incapable of mounting effective, large-scale, sustained operations.[4] The air force lacks significant in-flight refuelling capability, and so cannot protect the fleet outside the combat radius of land-based aircraft. China is unlikely to deploy an aircraft carrier for some time, and a full aircraft-carrier battle group capable of large-scale power projection is a very distant prospect.[5] Moreover, while generating vital finance, the PLA's heavy involvement in business has eroded morale and military effectiveness.[6]

Japan has substantially improved its military capabilities since the early 1980s, although stagnant defence spending has meant limited procurement since the mid-1990s. The fact that its armed forces are geared to defending against invasion, rather than projecting power, has also imposed limitations. Overall, the country's navy is the most modern, and the best-equipped, in Asia, but it suffers from several important weaknesses. In particular, it lacks ship-based air support, and its under-way supply and amphibious transport capacities are weak. The JDA has begun building a class of 8,900-tonne amphibious transport ships, which could carry *Harrier*-type combat aircraft as well as helicopters, and may be a first step towards developing an aircraft carrier.[7] The air force has no in-flight refuelling aircraft, no dedicated strike capability and only limited long-range air transport. The army lacks 'strategic or even major tactical mobility'.[8] Joint operations doctrine and integrated logistic support concepts are underdeveloped.[9]

Japan's key military strengths lie in its access to sophisticated technologies, and its ability to integrate them into operational equipment. In areas relevant to the RMA, particularly command, control, communications and computer-processing ($C^4$) and intelligence-collection, surveillance and reconnaissance (ISR), Japan is ahead of its East Asian neighbours. Tokyo has obtained some of the most advanced systems sold to US allies, such as the *Aegis* combat data system for its *Kongou*-class destroyers, and the latest AWACS aircraft.[10] The establishment of a centralised Defence Intelligence Headquarters in 1997, and the decision in November 1998 to launch Japan's first reconnaissance satellites, indicate a serious effort to improve intelligence collection, coordination and dissemination.[11] Legislation passed in April 1999 allows Japan to cooperate with US forces, not only against a direct attack, but also in undefined 'surrounding areas'. However, a more assertive defence posture is conceivable only if a profound change takes place in Japan's strategic circumstances, such as US military withdrawal from the region, or in the event of a major regional conflict.[12]

The defence programmes of other East Asian states do not have the wider significance of those of China and Japan, but are nonetheless important at a sub-regional level. Since the early 1980s, Taiwan's armed forces have been increasingly geared towards self-defence, rather than invading the Chinese mainland. Taipei's priority has been improving the capabilities of its navy and air force, with the stress on acquiring high-technology weapon systems. Improvements in $C^4$ include E-2 early-warning aircraft, the automated 'Strong Net' air-defence network, and the 'Software

Initiatives' programme of systems integration.[13] In January 1999, the first of three planned 'research satellites', widely believed to have military surveillance applications, was launched.[14] Perceived vulnerability to Chinese electronic and information warfare has prompted countermeasures, including setting up an air force electronic-warfare group.[15] Regular major exercises test joint-service capabilities, including C[4], electronic warfare, air defence and anti-submarine warfare.[16] Although the army is being reduced in size, reorganised and re-equipped, it still relies heavily on conscripts and reservists.[17] This is a serious weakness, particularly given the increased training requirements necessary to operate sophisticated equipment.[18] Recruiting and retaining adequate numbers of regular personnel, particularly air force officers, was difficult during the economic boom of the 1990s.[19] Scandals over arms acquisitions, and domestic political debate concerning Taiwan's future, have damaged military morale and undermined respect for the armed forces.[20]

China's own military deficiencies, Taiwan's superiority in many areas of defence technology and the willingness of the US to provide at least logistical support in the event of conflict make aggression by Beijing unlikely. More importantly, China is anxious to avoid bloodshed, and keen to integrate Taiwan economically intact. It is thus unlikely to try to defeat the island's air force and navy, to attempt amphibious or airborne landings, or to mount a naval blockade. Extreme circumstances, such as a Taiwanese declaration of independence, Taipei's development of nuclear weapons, or a breakdown in the island's domestic order, might compel Beijing to use these 'orthodox' options.[21] Nonetheless, 'unorthodox' attempts to intimidate Taiwan remain more likely. These include renewed large-scale military exercises and missile tests close to the island, which would emphasise Taiwan's vulnerability. Neither the *Patriot* PAC-II SAM deployed in 1998 nor the indigenous *Sky Bow* II system, due for deployment in 2000, is likely to provide a credible defence against Chinese missiles.[22]

During the 1990s, South Korea has sought to become more self-reliant in defence. The Force Improvement Program has looked beyond immediate security concerns over North Korea towards contingencies in which a future unified Korea might need to defend itself and its interests without US support. Since these interests include vital sea-lanes, Seoul has placed notable emphasis on improving naval power projection.[23] South Korea also seems intent on developing forces able to implement its own version of the RMA, particularly in precision targeting.[24] Air force procurement includes aircraft equipped for signals intelligence, *Popeye* air-launched missiles, HARM anti-radar missiles, and LANTIRN navigation and targeting equipment. There are also plans to launch a military communications and reconnaissance satellite in 2005.[25] Strenuous efforts have been made to improve $C^4$ and integrated logistic support throughout the armed forces.[26] New naval vessels are being equipped with modern tactical data systems; *Aegis* may be fitted to some planned KDX-2-class destroyers.

South Korea has clear conventional military advantages over its northern adversary. Although North Korea's armed forces are larger, and enjoy numerical superiority in many equipment categories, most of this equipment is outdated and ineffective. Seoul's forces are greatly superior in $C^4$ and ISR, logistics and training for large-scale, 24-hour operations. While South Korea's armed forces have their own training, morale and discipline problems, in the 1990s the North has had serious difficulties feeding and clothing its soldiers.[27] The close operational links between the 36,000-strong US forces in Korea and the South Korean military, and Washington's commitment to deploy significant reinforcements in the event of large-scale North Korean aggression, tilt the military balance on the Peninsula still further in the South's favour. However, even the near-inevitability of defeat might not deter a last-ditch attempt by a desperate North Korean regime to save itself by destroying the South.

Any North Korean offensive might involve strategies against which the South cannot be effectively defended. Seoul is only 50 kilometres from the demilitarised zone (DMZ), and is thus exposed to pre-emptive attack by *Frog* and *Scud* missiles armed with chemical, biological and, possibly, nuclear warheads. Multiple-rocket launchers and artillery could be used to direct massive volumes of high-explosive and chemical weapons against South Korean and US forces south of the DMZ. Before counter-battery fire, air attacks or a land counter-offensive neutralised North Korean delivery systems, immense harm could have been done to the South's civilian population and infrastructure, as well as to South Korean and US forces.[28]

For budgetary, political, educational and cultural reasons, most South-east Asian armed forces are less able to absorb the RMA than their North-east Asian counterparts. Although Malaysia and Thailand have tried to improve their C⁴ and ISR capabilities during the 1990s, South-east Asian armed forces have generally not begun the doctrinal, organisational and logistical revolutions required to take advantage of the RMA. Singapore is the only South-east Asian state to have moved significantly towards

*South-east Asia is further behind than North-east Asia in RMA terms*

developing RMA-type forces. The city-state's small population of around three million has meant that, to build a credible order of battle, the armed forces have relied on conscripts and reservists for the bulk of their personnel. But the military is built around a strong core of approximately 30,000 regulars, including a semi-professional air force and navy. Regulars, conscripts and reservists alike are well-trained and, in many cases, highly educated. Singapore has increasingly invested its growing defence budgets in high-technology systems. Since the mid-1980s, the armed forces have acquired sophisticated C⁴ and ISR assets which far outclass those available elsewhere in South-east Asia. These include E-2C AEW aircraft, Fokker 50s equipped for electronic intelligence as well as maritime patrol, RF-5S reconnaissance fighters, *Searcher* UAVs, and mobile air-defence radar. A local ground-station enables the armed forces to exploit commercial satellite imagery; in April 1999, Singaporean communications equipment was included in the payload of a British mini-satellite launched by Russia.[29] Singapore's new F-16C/D fighters are equipped with the LANTIRN system, and will be fitted with Israeli-made tactical datalink terminals.[30] Singapore has also implemented important organisational, doctrinal and logistical improvements. While these changes are insufficient to allow the RMA's full-scale adoption, they will reinforce Singapore's existing military advantages over its South-east Asian neighbours.

## Challenges to the Regional Balance

Military modernisation might make conflict more likely in East Asia. Greater power-projection capabilities could bring the forces of potential adversaries into more direct contact. China's increasing strategic reach might, for example, lead to clashes with South-east

Asian forces in the South China Sea. But those East Asian states building on their sub-regional or local conventional military advantages – Japan, South Korea, Singapore and Taiwan – are the region's most technologically advanced countries, with links to the US which allow wide access to critical RMA technologies. They are thus likely to be more successful than other states in improving their military capabilities, at least for the next decade, despite the impact of the economic crisis on their defence programmes. External threat perceptions, particularly in South Korea, Singapore and Taiwan, mean that defence spending is likely to be maintained. None of these countries is likely to use its burgeoning military capability aggressively. By East Asian standards, they are all relatively strong states, with more or less accountable systems of governance, and their foreign policies are predictably peaceful.

The overwhelming US lead in RMA capabilities, coupled with America's massive nuclear forces, suggests that Washington will remain the region's most important military power. Washington's forthright response to the 1996 Taiwan Straits crisis, and its later reinforcement of key regional alliances with Japan and Australia, suggest that any major change in its strategic posture is unlikely, at least in the medium term. In November 1998, Washington confirmed its 1995 commitment to maintain approximately 100,000 military personnel in East Asia.[31] Korean reunification could undermine the rationale for maintaining US forces in the South and in Japan, but this is not imminent. Two critical developments could nonetheless diminish the conventional military advantages of the US and its regional allies. The first is the increasing importance in the region of WMD and associated long-range delivery systems.[32] The second is the likelihood that China will eventually develop its own version of the RMA.

### WMD and Missiles

Japan, South Korea and Taiwan all have the technical potential to develop nuclear weapons and long-range missiles, but are constrained from doing so by their close security relations with the US, their adherence to international agreements and, for Japan especially, domestic political factors. Both South Korea and Taiwan have indicated that they are able to develop long-range ballistic missiles, and both could reactivate their frozen nuclear-weapon programmes.[33]

However, these latent capabilities are essentially insurance policies against any weakening of US security commitments.

States with relatively unsophisticated conventional forces may see WMD and related missile systems as effective counters to RMA-rich adversaries. Thus, North Korea and China pose the key WMD and missile challenges in the region. Under the Agreed Framework of 1994, the US, South Korea, Japan and the EU are committed to supplying fuel oil and civilian nuclear-power stations to Pyongyang, which undertook to freeze its nuclear-weapon programme in exchange. Nonetheless, international concerns will probably persist as long as the regime remains in power. An agreement reached in March 1999, allowing the US to inspect the Kumchangri underground research facility, has not convinced observers that the North has abandoned its nuclear-weapon programme.[34] Apart from its nuclear potential, Pyongyang is believed to possess large quantities of chemical and biological weapons.[35]

Evidence of Pyongyang's missile development is more clear-cut. By 1998, North Korea had deployed not only extensively modified, 320km- and 500km-range versions of Russian *Scud* missiles, but probably also the *Nodong*, which, with a range of over 1,000km, is capable of reaching many parts of Japan, including major US bases.[36] In addition, *Taepodong* missiles with ranges of over 1,500km and 4,000km are being developed. A three-stage *Taepodong* was test-launched over Japan in August 1998.[37] In December 1998, it was reported that North Korea was building underground *Taepodong* launch sites.[38] North Korea also produces Chinese-designed *Silkworm* cruise missiles, and is developing more advanced *Silkworm* derivatives.[39] While North Korea's missiles may be inaccurate, they could be effective weapons if armed with nuclear, chemical or biological warheads. North Korea could use its missiles and WMD to strike US bases and other targets in Japan. If the longer-range *Taepodong* missiles were operational, they could reach Alaska, Guam and the far west of the Hawaiian chain; with smaller payloads, they could even reach the continental US.[40] The fact that this would almost certainly trigger the use of US nuclear weapons might not deter a desperate regime in Pyongyang.

During the 1990s, Chinese sources have emphasised that modernising long-range missile forces is a priority. The PLA's focus on winning limited or local wars under high-technology conditions is predicated on modernising China's nuclear, as well as conventional, forces. Since the late 1980s, Beijing's nuclear doctrine has apparently evolved from minimum deterrence (threatening a second strike against enemy cities) to what PLA strategists refer to as 'limited deterrence' – limited nuclear war-fighting with wider options in terms of the conditions for and timing of nuclear use, postulating 'a mix of hard and soft counterforce and countervalue targets'.[41] Weaknesses in China's nuclear forces, particularly in missile guidance systems, as well as the relatively small number of warheads deployed, imply that a limited war-fighting capability will be unattainable for some years. However, during the 1990s there have been numerous indications that China's programme of nuclear modernisation has been structured around limited deterrence. This has included enlarging its ICBM force, and developing:[42]

- DF-31 and -41 mobile, solid-fuel ICBMs, and the JL-2 submarine-launched ballistic missile (SLBM);
- longer-range versions of the DF-21 intermediate-range ballistic missile;
- multiple independently targetable re-entry vehicle warheads;
- miniaturised warheads;
- improved ICBM/SLBM guidance (probably with Russian assistance);
- new theatre ballistic missiles such as the DF-15;
- improved mobility for existing DF-3 theatre ballistic missiles;
- strategic land-attack and other cruise missiles; and
- naval tactical nuclear weapons.

Despite its much-vaunted nuclear no-first-use policy, China's modernisation of its nuclear weapons and long-range missiles may enable Beijing to deter US intervention in future regional security crises by threatening nuclear escalation. This applies most obviously to US action to protect Taiwan from Chinese blockades or other intimidation. Increasing the number of short-range ballistic missiles deployed against Taiwan, and augmenting them with cruise missiles, would give China more options for conventional, as well as nuclear, warfare.[43]

Since the early 1990s, there has been considerable interest – particularly in the US Congress and in the Pentagon – in deploying national missile defence (NMD) systems to defend the continental US, and in jointly developing TMD to protect Japan and South Korea. NMD and TMD systems would be designed to neutralise threats such as those posed by Chinese and North Korean missiles and WMD, thereby maintaining the credibility of Washington's security guarantees and allowing the conventional military superiority of the US and its North-east Asian allies to prevail. However, although North Korea's *Taepodong* test in August 1998 increased funding for US NMD and TMD development, the deployment of effective systems is not a foregone conclusion. The US government will not decide until 2000 if or when to deploy NMD, and no deployment will take place before 2005.[44] Pyongyang's test also prompted a US House of Representatives' vote requiring the Pentagon to study the feasibility of including 'key regional allies' (Japan, South Korea and Taiwan) in a TMD network.[45] Although in late 1998 Tokyo decided to fund joint research with the US into TMD, Japanese Prime Minister Keizo Obuchi noted that the programme would take more than ten years and would need massive investment, while 100% effectiveness was not guaranteed.[46] Given these concerns, along with US reluctance to pass on relevant technology, Taiwan has resisted committing itself to the project.[47] Nonetheless, in 1998 Taipei revealed a ten-year national programme to deploy anti-missile systems, and requested from the US destroyers equipped with the *Aegis* system (a key element in US TMD plans), as well as early-warning radar and additional *Patriot* missiles.[48] In March 1999, South Korean Defence Minister Chun Yong Taek ruled out participation in the TMD programme on the grounds that it would not provide an effective defence against the short-range missiles that threaten the South. Seoul is going ahead with its own anti-missile system.[49]

## China and the RMA

The PLA leadership seems intent on ensuring that China will not be a military pushover in the event of a regional conflict, and younger military leaders and strategists are acutely aware of the importance of the RMA.[50] Some military analysts recognise that, because of low defence spending, lack of high-technology equipment and poorly educated military personnel, the disparity between China's military capabilities and those of 'other relevant countries' – including the US, Japan, Taiwan and the states of the Association of South-East Asian Nations (ASEAN) – is increasing.[51] However, the PLA is still massive, and personnel costs continue to hobble efforts to modernise it.[52] Resource constraints limit the PLA's access to sophisticated weapons and related technology, and bureaucratic and cultural obstacles may hamper efforts to exploit imported technology. Most aspects of China's military R&D, production technologies and weapon systems lag at least a decade behind those of the West. China's main foreign source of technology, Russia, is particularly weak in many areas crucial to the RMA.[53] The PLA's joint-operations doctrine and practice are underdeveloped, $C^4$ and ISR capabilities are generally outdated and logistical support is 'largely inadequate for distant or sophisticated operations'.[54]

These shortcomings notwithstanding, reforms in China's defence R&D and procurement organisations may mean that an 'RMA with Chinese characteristics' may be emerging.[55] China's embryonic RMA emphasises the development of 'a wide range of space and ground-based sensors to cue long-range precision strike assets and provide advanced warning of impending attacks'.[56] The PLA is rectifying its $C^4$ and ISR weaknesses, particularly by developing military space capabilities.[57] China is also developing its submarine force, and anti-ship submarine-launched cruise missiles are likely to be deployed in the near future. Other systems under development include surface- and air-launched missiles designed to engage AWACS and radar-jamming aircraft, and anti-satellite laser weapons.[58]

## Prospects for the Regional Balance

The regime in Pyongyang is unlikely to endure, limiting the longer-term significance of North Korea's missile and WMD programmes. Whether China's growing military power will significantly increase the likelihood of conflict is a more complex question. The regional military balance, in which US preponderance plays a vital role, is one of the key elements assuring regional peace. But over the next two decades, the military advantages of the US and its East Asian allies could erode.

Some observers place great hope on creating a rules-based regional security architecture founded on responsible and restrained international behaviour. Developing such a structure, however, depends on whether strong, stable states, enjoying domestic social and political cohesion and prosperous, resilient economies, become the norm. Only when they predominate and set the tone for the region's international relations can East Asia develop the strong economic and security regimes which will best guarantee regional peace and prosperity. China's political, as well as economic, development is particularly important. But this suggests a gradual, long-term process; the regional military balance may become less stable before nascent regimes have become sufficiently institutionalised and influential to manage and reduce the potential for conflict.

Since the late 1980s, growing prosperity and unabated insecurity have encouraged East Asian governments to devote substantial resources to modernising their armed forces. Since 1997, however, the economic crisis has curtailed defence spending in several states. Although China, Japan, South Korea, Singapore and Taiwan are likely to remain major international purchasers, the economic downturn has disappointed defence suppliers. Even before the crisis, the regional arms market was extremely competitive, with Western European, Russian and Israeli companies challenging US dominance throughout the 1990s. Strategic, economic and political links have remained important factors in East Asia's procurement decisions, while the willingness to pass on technology has sometimes been decisive. Competition between suppliers and the continued interest of East Asian governments in military modernisation mean that arms-control measures currently in force or under discussion are unlikely to have a significant impact on the flow of conventional weapons to the region. Prevailing economic conditions will have a far greater effect on the scale of arms transfers to East Asia.

While the East Asian market will remain important for outside suppliers, regional states will continue to develop their own defence industries. However, dependence on foreign technology and know-how and the small size of domestic markets have hampered progress towards self-reliance. Although 'spin-on' from high-technology civilian industries has helped in Japan and South Korea, across the region national defence industries are weak in systems-integration skills, making it difficult for most states to absorb many aspects of the RMA. Attempts to diversify into civilian production or to win export markets have also met with only limited success. Nevertheless, previously state-dominated defence industries have become more commercial, the private sector has become more involved, and co-production, joint ventures and foreign investment have widened international links. The economic crisis is likely to increase this international collaboration as the need for capital, technology and markets grows. The restructuring of defence industries is also likely to accelerate in the worst-hit countries. Developing and producing major systems may seem less feasible, both financially and technologically. But in East Asia's more advanced states, 'spin-on' may help local industries to play increasingly significant roles as suppliers of sub-systems and components, and as joint-venture partners.

Those East Asian armed forces best placed to benefit from the RMA will enjoy notable conventional military advantages over less advanced neighbours, though the region's most technologically developed states are unlikely to use their burgeoning military capacities aggressively. The substantial US lead in developing the RMA suggests that America's conventional forces will continue to outclass those of its likely East Asian adversaries for at least the next decade. However, Chinese and North Korean missile and WMD programmes may cause problems for the US and its allies. Missile defences may not provide a timely, affordable, effective or politically acceptable solution. An emergent 'RMA with Chinese characteristics' could negate the military advantages of the US and its regional allies by giving the PLA accurate and destructive, but relatively cheap, systems with which to threaten high-value platforms such as aircraft carriers.

Given these possibilities, other factors – political pluralisation and the creation of regional security regimes – must play a greater role if peace is to be preserved in the longer term. In the meantime, East Asian states will continue to see accumulating military power as an attractive way to protect and promote their interests. Some, particularly in South-east Asia, may be unable to afford the military modernisation planned in the early and mid-1990s. But the region's most significant military players – China, Japan, South Korea, Singapore and Taiwan – are likely to continue building modern, powerful and increasingly capable forces.

*notes*

## Acknowledgements

The authors would like to thank Sally Harris for her research assistance, and David Hughes, Ron Matthews and Harumi Yoshino for their advice and comments.

## Definitions and Data

This paper defines East Asia as comprising China, Japan, the two Koreas, Taiwan and the ten Southeast Asian states. Not all East Asian governments release accurate or comparable figures for their defence spending, and only estimates are available for several key states, including China and Indonesia. Myanmar, Singapore and Vietnam do not publish breakdowns of their defence budgets; in Brunei, Indonesia, Malaysia and the Philippines, a large proportion of procurement funding derives from special grants, development plans or non-budgetary sources.

## Chapter 1

[1] *The Military Balance, 1997/98* (Oxford: Oxford University Press for the IISS, 1998), p. 295; *SIPRI Yearbook 1997* (Oxford: Oxford University Press for the Stockholm International Peace Research Institute (SIPRI), 1997), p. 197.
[2] Actual Indonesian expenditure may be two or three times higher than official figures suggest.
[3] *The Military Balance 1997/98*, p. 295.
[4] Sinfah Tunsarawuth, 'Shopping Spree for Thailand's Armed Forces May Be on Hold', *Straits Times*, 13 June 1996; Jaime Carrera, 'Battle to Beat Military Cuts', *Bangkok Post*, 27 April 1997.
[5] Edward Tang, 'Chuan Sees Role for Private Sector in Military', *Straits Times*, 1 December 1997; Nate Thayer and Charles Bickers, 'Market Misfire', *Far Eastern Economic Review*, 5 February 1998, p. 22.
[6] 'Army Seeks to Delay Arms Purchase Payments', *Asian Defence Journal*, February 1998, p. 69.

[7] 'Jet Saga Draws to a Close', *Bangkok Post*, 8 May 1998.

[8] Thayer and Bickers, 'Market Misfire', p. 22; Paul Lewis, 'Hornets Nest', *Flight International*, 22 April 1998, pp. 28–29.

[9] 'Thais Juggle UAV Payment', *Asian Defence Journal*, October 1998, p. 64.

[10] Ted Bardacke, 'Cash-Tight Military in Thailand Shows Its Might to Tourists', *Financial Times*, 6–7 March 1999.

[11] 'Cabinet Approves B825 Billion', *Bangkok Post*, 27 May 1998, p. 3; 'Thai Spending Boost Considered', *Jane's Defence Weekly*, 28 April 1999, p. 15.

[12] *Berita Harian*, 22 April 1998, in *BBC Summary of World Broadcasts, The Far East* (SWB/FE) 3208 B/6, 23 April 1998.

[13] 'KL Slashes Defence Expenditure', *Straits Times*, 15 March 1999.

[14] *Radio Australia*, 29 November 1997, in SWB/FE 3090 B/2, 1 December 1997; 'Malaysia File', *Straits Times*, 28 April 1998; Andrzej Jeziorski, 'Malaysia Backpedals on CN-235 Buy and Postpones AEW Procurement for Five Years', *Flight International*, 29 April 1998, p. 22.

[15] Prasun K. Sengupta, 'Contract Signed for First Six NGPVs for RMN', *Asian Defence Journal*, March 1999, pp. 6–7.

[16] 'Philippines' $13b Force Modernization Plan', *Straits Times*, 28 April 1998.

[17] Steven Watkins, 'Philippines May Juggle Modernization Priorities', *Defense News*, 10 August 1998, pp. 4, 20.

[18] 'AFP Modernisation Takes Off at Last', *Asian Defence Journal*, May 1999, p. 62.

[19] *Angkatan Bersenjata*, 8 January 1998, in SWB/FE 3121 B/4, 10 January 1998.

[20] Thalif Deen, 'Indonesia Postpones Planned Arms Purchases', *Jane's Defence Weekly*, 21 October 1998, p. 21.

[21] *Radio Republic of Indonesia*, 14 January 1998, in SWB/FE 3125 B/2, 15 January 1998.

[22] Steven Lee Myers, 'Arms Makers Scramble to Keep Asia Contracts', *International Herald Tribune*, 14 January 1998, p. 7; John Haseman, 'Indonesia Cuts Back on Spending as Crisis Bites', *Jane's Defence Weekly*, 21 January 1998, p. 6; ITAR-TASS, 26 July 1998, in SWB/FE 3290 B/8, 28 July 1998.

[23] 'Intelligence', *Far Eastern Economic Review*, 20 August 1998, p. 8.

[24] 'Indonesia Cancels Contracts', *Air Forces Monthly*, April 1999, p. 16.

[25] *The Military Balance 1997/98*, p. 167.

[26] Paul Lewis, 'South Korea Considers Plan to Extend Production of F-16s', *Flight International*, 3–9 September 1997, p. 17.

[27] *Yonhap News Agency*, 24 July 1998, in SWB/FE 3288 D/4, 25 July 1998; *The Military Balance 1998/99* (Oxford: Oxford University Press for the IISS, 1998), p. 169.

[28] Andrzej Jeziorski, 'Cash Shortage Threatens More Procurement Delays in S. Korea', *Flight International*, 27 January 1999, p. 25; Robert Karniol, 'S. Korea Plans to Spend $6.35b Up To 2004', *Jane's Defence Weekly*, 24 February 1999, p. 4.

[29] *Yonhap News Agency*, 6 January 1998, in SWB/FE 3119 D/3, 8 January 1998; Robert Karniol, 'South Korea Postpones Programmes Amid Crisis', *Jane's Defence Weekly*, 21 January 1998, p. 14; Barbara Opall, 'Seoul's KTX-2 Enters Final Development', *Defense News*, 1 December 1997, pp. 28, 30; *Choson Ilbo*, 6 January 1998, in SWB/FE 3119 D/4, 8 January 1998;

Paul Lewis, 'Partners Rearrange KTX-II Schedule after Budget Cuts', *Flight International*, 22 April 1998, p. 16.

[30] Karniol, 'S. Korea Plans to Spend $6.35b'.

[31] *The Military Balance 1997/98*, p. 166.

[32] *Kyodo News Service*, 28 April 1997, in SWB/FE 2905 E/1, 29 April 1997; Kwan Weng Kin, 'Japan to Cut Defence Spending by $11b Over Next Three Years', *Straits Times*, 4 June 1997; *Kyodo News Service*, 18 December 1997, in SWB/FE 3107 E/2, 20 December 1997.

[33] *Kyodo News Service*, 20 August 1997, in SWB/FE 3006 E/3, 25 August 1997; Naoaki Usui, 'Japan's Parliament Is Likely to Accept '98 Defense Budget', *Defense News*, 26 January 1998, p. 24; Paul Lewis, 'JDA May Focus on Tanker and Transport', *Flight International*, 6 May 1998, p. 24.

[34] Kensuke Ebata, 'Japan Puts Off Decision on Missile Defence Plan', *Jane's Defence Weekly*, 18 June 1997, p. 15.

[35] 'Japan, US Agree to Join in Missile Defense System', *Washington Times*, 26 December 1998, p. 10; Andrez Jeziorski, 'Japan Considers Tanker Buy', *Flight International*, 13 January 1999, p. 19.

[36] Robert Karniol, 'Troop Strength Cuts Add to Rising Chinese Budget', *Jane's Defence Weekly*, 11 March 1998, p. 5.

[37] *The Military Balance 1998/99*, p. 178. For a detailed discussion, see 'China's Military Expenditure', in *The Military Balance 1995/96* (Oxford: Oxford University Press for the IISS, 1995), pp. 270–75.

[38] On China's claims, see *China: Arms Control and Disarmament* (Beijing: Information Office of the State Council, 1995), pp. 11–12. For assessments of funding outside the official budget, see *The Military Balance 1995/96*, pp. 272–73; You Ji, 'High-Tech Shift for China's Military', *Asian Defence Journal*, September 1995, p. 7; Karniol, 'Troop Strength Cuts'. Some sources claim that all procurement and research and development is funded from outside the defence budget. See, for example, Eric Arnett, 'Military Technology: The Case of China', *SIPRI Yearbook 1995* (Oxford: Oxford University Press for SIPRI, 1995), p. 327.

[39] *The Military Balance 1997/98*, p. 167.

[40] Naoaki Usui, 'Chi Says Defense Budget Yields to Economy', *Defense News*, 9 February 1998, p. 40.

[41] Karniol, 'Troop Strength Cuts', p. 5.

[42] *Cheng Ming*, Hong Kong, in SWB/FE 3450 G/4, 4 February 1999.

[43] See James Kynge, 'China's Military "Complete Business Empire Handover"', *Financial Times*, 15 December 1998, p. 8.

[44] John Pomfret, 'China's Army Feels Bite of Reforms', *International Herald Tribune*, 20 August 1998, p. 4; Mary Kwang, 'Be Thrifty, China's Army Told', *Straits Times*, 9 March 1999.

[45] *1998 National Defense Report: Republic of China* (Taipei: Li Ming Cultural Enterprise Co Ltd for the Ministry of National Defence, 1998), p. 123.

[46] Figures from Taiwan's Ministry of National Defence, June 1998; Mure Dickie, 'Taiwan Approves Budget', *Financial Times*, 31 May 1999, p. 4.

[47] *Central News Agency*, Taipei, 30 September 1997, in SWB/FE 3039 F/3-4, 2 October 1997; 'USA Considers Taiwanese Sale', *Jane's Defence Weekly*, 4 February 1998, p. 11; *Central News Agency*, 5 February

1998, in SWB/FE 3146 F/3, 9 February 1998; *ibid.*, 8 March 1998, in SWB/FE 3171 F/2, 10 March 1998; Christopher Foss, 'Taiwan Gets M109A5s', *Jane's Defence Weekly*, 15 April 1998, p. 20; '10-Year Taiwan Arms Plan to Counter China', *Straits Times*, 13 July 1998; Bryan Bender and Robert Karniol, 'Taiwan Puts $600m into Missile Programmes', *Jane's Defence Weekly*, 10 March 1999, p. 4.

[48] Ravi Velloor, 'Dr Hu Unveils Prudent Budget', *Straits Times Weekly Edition*, 28 February 1998, p. 1.

[49] Speech by Dr Tony Tan Keng Yam, Deputy Prime Minister and Minister for Defence, 7 January 1998, *Media Releases*, MINDEF Internet Service.

[50] Barbara Opall, 'Big Wishes, Slim Budgets Drive Asian Buys', *Defense News*, 10–16 November 1997, p. 26.

[51] See Jeffrey Sachs, 'Glimmers of Hope', *Far Eastern Economic Review*, 5 November 1998, p. 53; 'Growth Signals Asian Recovery', *International Herald Tribune*, 3–4 April 1999.

[52] 'Asia's Shallow Recovery', *Financial Times*, 6 April 1999.


**Chapter 2**

[1] *The Military Balance 1997/98*, p. 265; *The Military Balance 1998/99*, p. 272.

[2] Barbara Opall, 'US Industry Urges More IMF Aid for E. Asia', *Defense News*, 2 February 1998, p. 19.

[3] *SIPRI Yearbook 1998*, p. 300.

[4] *The Military Balance 1997/98*, p. 265; *The Military Balance 1998/99*, p. 270.

[5] 'US Military Exports to China More Damaging than Thefts: Report', *Asian Defence Journal*, May 1999, p. 64.

[6] In June 1998, for example, China's Foreign Ministry condemned the proposed US sale of navigation and targeting pods for Taiwan's F-16 fighters. According to the official Chinese press, the sale violated Sino-US agreements, as well as China's sovereignty. *Zhongguo Xinwen She News Agency* (Beijing), 4 June 1998, in SWB/FE 3246 F/1, 6 June 1998.

[7] *Lien Ho Pao*, Taiwan, 31 March 1998, in SWB/FE 3192 F/1, 3 April 1998.

[8] *Central News Agency*, 7 January 1997, in SWB/FE 2811 F/2, 8 January 1997.

[9] Bryan Bender, 'Legislation Aims to Boost US Arms Sales to Taiwan', *Jane's Defence Weekly*, 14 April 1999, p. 5.

[10] See 'Singapore Aims to Pull US Strings for Longbow', *Flight International*, 28 October 1998, p. 22; 'Air Force Takes Aim at AMRAAM', *Asian Defence Journal*, October 1998, p. 63.

[11] Joel Johnson, quoted in Barbara Opall, 'Europeans to Gain Ground in European Arms Markets', *Defense News*, 24 June 1996, p. 63.

[12] David Vadas, quoted in Barbara Opall, 'Asia Is Top US Market for Aerospace Exports', *ibid.*, 28 July 1997, p. 6.

[13] 'Row over US Defense Mart Guide Aggravated', *Korea Times*, 18 April 1998.

[14] Carol Reed, Robert Karniol and Ron Matthews, 'South Korean Business: Diversify for Survival', *Jane's Defence Weekly*, 31 July 1993, pp. 15–16. On the changing South Korean defence market, see Paul Abrahms, 'South Korea Survey: Europe's Chance – The Defence Market Opens', *Financial Times*, 23 June 1994.

[15] Robert Karniol, 'Interview: Lt-Gen William Hotchkiss, Commanding General, Philippine Air Force', *Jane's Defence Weekly*, 20

May 1998, p. 32.

[16] Barbara Opall, 'Indonesia Doubts US Fidelity as Arms Source', *Defense News*, 23 February 1998, p. 3.

[17] Paul Lewis, 'Future Fighter Needs', *Flight International*, 18 February 1998, p. 64.

[18] See Malcolm Chalmers, *British Arms Export Policy and Indonesia* (London: Saferworld, 1997), p. 33.

[19] Between 1993 and 1997, 47% of British defence exports were delivered to the Middle East, particularly Saudi Arabia. Defence Export Services Organisation (DESO), September 1998.

[20] Richard Norton-Taylor, 'Ministers "Broke Law on Pergau"', *The Guardian*, 10 November 1994.

[21] Paul Lewis, 'Brunei Clears Decks for BAe Deal', *Flight International*, 28 January 1998, p. 19; 'Brunei Orders Three British Patrol Vessels', *Defense News*, 2 February 1998, p. 9.

[22] DESO, June 1997 and March 1998.

[23] Sadaaki Numata, 'The Role of Japan in Regional and World Security', *RUSI Journal*, vol. 142, no. 4, August 1997, pp. 15–16.

[24] 'S. Korea to Spend $118b on Defence', *Straits Times*, 15 February 1999.

[25] J. A. C. Lewis, 'French Arms Exports Reach Decade High', *Jane's Defence Weekly*, 1 July 1998, p. 23.

[26] Peter Lewis, 'Deal Rules Out Taiwan as French Market', *ibid.*, 29 January 1994, p. 11.

[27] *Ibid.*; Paul Beaver, 'First Two La Fayettes Sail for Taiwan', *Jane's Defence Weekly*, 20 March 1996, p. 14; 'France to Honour Arms Deals with Taiwan', *Straits Times*, 12 December 1996; Barbara Opall, 'Copter Builders Chase Taiwan Market', *Defense News*, 18 August 1997, p. 20.

[28] 'France Returns', *Asian Military Review*, December 1995–January 1996, p. 63; 'French Arms Sales Veto after Mirage Deliveries', *World Air Power Journal*, vol. 30, Autumn 1997, p. 11.

[29] *Xinhua News Agency*, 22 January 1998, in SWB/FE 3132 G/1, 23 January 1998; 'Taiwan Receives French ATGWs', *Jane's Defence Weekly*, 22 July 1998, p. 14.

[30] Jon Lake, 'Air Power Analysis: Taiwan', *World Air Power Journal*, vol. 33, Summer 1998, p. 152.

[31] Jon Sparks, 'Technology Transplants for the PLAN', *Jane's International Defense Review*, February 1989, p. 165; *SIPRI Yearbook 1997*, p. 302; *Jane's Fighting Ships 1998–99* (Coulsdon, Surrey: Jane's Information Group, 1998), pp. 117–18.

[32] 'Malaysia Signs Double Deals for OPV Contract', *Jane's Defence Weekly*, 25 February 1998, p. 16.

[33] Hanns W. Maull, 'Reconciling China with International Order', *Pacific Review*, vol. 10, no. 4, 1997, p. 471; *Central News Agency*, 4 February 1997, in SWB/FE 2836 F/6, 6 February 1997; 'German Torpedoes Backfire', *Borneo Bulletin*, 3 December 1997; Robert Karniol, 'Country Briefing: Taiwan', *Jane's Defence Weekly*, 8 July 1998, p. 25; and *Jane's Fighting Ships 1997–98* (Coulsdon, Surrey: Jane's Information Group, 1997), p. 695; Damian Kemp, 'China May Hit Dasa over Development of High-Resolution Satellite for Taiwan', *Jane's Defence Weekly*, 14 April 1999, p. 22.

[34] *Jane's Fighting Ships 1998–99*, p. 118.

[35] Brian Cloughley, 'Japan Ponders Power Projection', *Jane's International Defense Review*, July 1996, p. 29.

[36] Hugh Williamson, 'Red–Green Signals', *Far Eastern Economic Review*, 12 November 1998, p. 28.

[37] 'Statement of the Deputy Prime Minister and Minister for Defence, Dr Tony Tan, Following the Launch of the Submarine RSS *Challenger* at Malmo, Sweden', *Media Releases*, MINDEF Internet Service, 26 September 1997.

[38] *Jane's Fighting Ships 1998–99*, p. 622.

[39] Richard Bassett, 'No Single Step to Euro Aerospace Merger', *Jane's Defence Weekly*, 25 November 1998, p. 21.

[40] Interview with Vance Coffman, Chairman, Lockheed Martin, *ibid.*, 18 November 1998, p. 32.

[41] *Defense News*, 28 April 1997, p. 1.

[42] See Alexander A. Sergounin and Sergey V. Subbotin, 'Sino-Russian Military–Technical Cooperation: A Russian View', in Ian Anthony (ed.), *Russia and the Arms Trade* (Oxford: Oxford University Press for SIPRI, 1998), pp. 194–96.

[43] *ITAR-TASS*, 12 December 1996, in SWB/FE 2795 G/1–2, 14 December 1996.

[44] Douglas Barrie, 'Coming Down to Earth', *Flight International*, 6 August 1997, p. 36.

[45] Sergounin and Subbotin, 'Sino-Russian Military–Technical Cooperation', pp. 197–98; 'China Seeks S-300 and Tor-M1 Systems', *Jane's Defence Weekly*, 2 September 1998, p. 16.

[46] 'Beijing Builds Su-27 Fighters from Russian Kits', *ibid.*, 10 June 1998, p. 12.

[47] Nikolai Novichkov, 'Russia and China Tighten Links on Military Projects', *ibid.*, 19 August 1998, p. 3; 'Russian 1.44 to Fly Soon, Says MAPO', *Flight International*, 20 January 1999.

[48] *Central News Agency*, 13 May 1996, in SWB/FE 2612 F/2, 15 May 1996.

[49] Christopher Bluth, 'Russia and China Consolidate Their New Strategic Partnership', *Jane's Intelligence Review*, August 1998, pp. 20–21.

[50] Barbara Opall-Rome, 'DoD Fights China's Pursuit of "Nuke" Furnace', *Defense News*, 27 April 1998, p. 1.

[51] See Alexander Velovich, 'Russians Consider Industry Restructure', *Flight International*, 27 January 1999, p. 8.

[52] See Jennifer Anderson, *The Limits of Sino-Russian Strategic Partnership*, Adelphi Paper 315 (Oxford: Oxford University Press for the IISS, 1997), p. 75; Nikolay Novichkov, 'Russian Arms Technology Pouring into China', *Aviation Week and Space Technology*, 12 May 1997, pp. 72–73; Paul Lewis, 'Russia Reviews Chinese Sales', *Flight International*, 17 September 1997, p. 21.

[53] 'Sukhoi Production Deal Criticised in Russia', *World Air Power Journal*, vol. 28, Spring 1997, p. 9.

[54] John Zeng, 'The New Sino-Russian Partnership: SU-27s the Icing on the Cake', *Asia-Pacific Defence Reporter*, May–June 1996, p. 13.

[55] Sergounin and Subbotin, 'Sino-Russian Military–Technical Cooperation', p. 196.

[56] *ITAR-TASS*, 30 September 1997, in SWB/FE 3039 F/4, 2 October 1997.

[57] *Sisa Journal*, 4 May 1995, in Foreign Broadcast Information Service (FBIS), *Daily Report*, EAS-95-086, 4 May 1995, p. 30; Robert Karniol, 'Russian Tanks to Bolster South Korean Forces', *Jane's Defence Weekly*, 21 February 1996, p. 15.

[58] *Yonhap News Agency*, 11 January 1998, in SWB/FE 3122 D/2, 12 January 1998.

[59] James Meek, 'Spies Enter Rocket Dogfight', *The Guardian*, 6 August 1997; 'SAM-X Feared to Be Potential Pandora's Box', *Korea*

*Times*, 6 June 1998.

[60] *Jane's Fighting Ships 1997–98*, p. 870.

[61] 'Yeltsin Visit to Boost Arms Sales', *Asian Defence Journal*, October 1998, pp. 64–65; 'RF Will Retain Its Naval Presence in Vietnam', *Nezavisaia Gazeta*, 22 October 1998, in *Northeast Asia Peace and Security Daily Report*, 26 October 1998.

[62] Piotr Butowski, 'Thrust Vectoring Will Drive MiG-29 Exports', *Jane's Defence Weekly*, 21 May 1997, p. 29.

[63] Piotr Butowski, '"Fulcrum" Will Fly Export Flag Beyond 2005', *ibid.*, 14 May 1997, p. 4.

[64] *RIA*, Moscow, 6 April 1999, in SWB/FE 3505 B/5, 10 April 1999.

[65] Steve Rodan, 'Israeli Firms Set Sights on Asia-Pacific Defense Market', *Defense News*, 9 June 1997, p. 6.

[66] E. Kogan, 'The Israeli Defence Industry Presence in the East Asian Market', *Asian Defence Journal*, April 1995, p. 36.

[67] Yitzhak Shichor, 'Israel's Military Transfers to China and Taiwan', *Survival*, vol. 40, no. 1, Spring 1998, p. 70.

[68] *Ibid.*, pp. 74, 80–81; Paul Lewis, 'Israel/Russia Compete to Arm F-10 Fighter', *Flight International*, 15 October 1997, p. 9; Steve Rodan, 'IAI, Russian Industries Seek to Wed Tech, Old Platforms', *Defense News*, 16 February 1998, p. 22.

[69] Barbara Opall, 'Israeli Defence Business Shifts from Taiwan to China', *Defense News*, 2 September 1996, p. 6.

[70] Ed Blanche, 'Israel Finds Changing Arms Market in China', *Jane's Defence Weekly*, 16 September 1998, p. 5.

[71] Shichor, 'Israel's Military Transfers', pp. 72–73.

[72] Kogan, 'The Israeli Defence Industry', p. 35.

[73] Barbara Opall, 'Sellers Exercise Flexibility Amid Asian Money Bind', *Defense News*, 2 March 1998, p. 20.

[74] Desmond Ball, *Developments in Signals Intelligence and Electronic Warfare in Southeast Asia*, Working Paper 290 (Canberra: Australian National University (ANU) Strategic and Defence Studies Centre, 1995), pp. 16–17; Douglas Barrie, 'Singaporean F-16D Block 52s Reveal Israeli Design Heritage', *Flight International*, 22 April 1998, p. 15; Tamir Eshel and Damian Kemp, 'Singapore Company in UAV Deal with Israel', *Jane's Defence Weekly*, 2 December 1998, p. 6.

[75] 'Malaysia, S. Africa Sign Defence Cooperation MoU', *Bernama News Agency*, Kuala Lumpur, 13 November 1996; 'Rooivalks for Malaysia', *Jane's Defence Weekly*, 1 July 1998, p. 7; Prasun K. Sengupta, 'South African Defence Industry in Asia-Pacific', *Asian Defence Journal*, November 1998, p. 23.

[76] Douglas Barrie, 'A Matter of Priorities', *Flight International*, 10 June 1998, p. 40.

[77] See Andrew Selth, *Burma's Arms Procurement Programme*, Working Paper 289 (Canberra: ANU Strategic and Defence Studies Centre, 1995), pp. 5–6, 31–32.

[78] Robert Karniol, 'Vietnam Stocking Up Scuds', *Jane's Defence Weekly*, 14 April 1999, p. 17.

[79] Hugh Williamson, 'German Torpedoes Backfire', *Borneo Bulletin*, 3 December 1997.

[80] Selth, *Burma's Arms Procurement Programme*, pp. 6–7, 14, 32.

[81] See Reinhard Drifte, *The Japanese–Korean High-Technology Relationship: Implications for Weapons Proliferation and Arms Control Regimes*, Occasional Paper 31 (Stockholm: Stockholm University Centre for Pacific Asia Studies, 1997).

[82] 'Malaysia Promotes Local Defence Contractors', *Jane's Defence Weekly Defence Industry Report*, May 1998, p. 2.

[83] 'Taiwanese Admiral', *Jane's Defence Weekly*, 13 May 1995, p. 5.

[84] *Central News Agency*, 18 March 1998, in SWB/FE 3180 F/1, 20 March 1998; *ibid.*, 19 March 1998, in SWB/FE 3181 F/1-2, 21 March 1998; Paul Webster, 'Fraud Inquiry Puts France on Brink of Constitution Crisis', *The Guardian*, 29 April 1998.

[85] John Burton, 'Roh Likely to Be Arrested for Bribes', *Financial Times*, 7 November 1995; 'South Korean Prosecutors Reopen Chun Bribe Inquiry', *The Times*, 12 December 1995; 'Seoul Shaken as Ex-Presidents Are Charged with Insurrection', *Jane's Defence Weekly*, 10 January 1996, p. 15.

[86] 'RoK Reconsiders Hawker Buy', *ibid.*, 21 October 1998, p. 21.

[87] 'Korean Defence Minister Promises Reforms', *Asian Defence Journal*, April 1998, pp. 103–104; *Phuchatkan*, 6 February 1998, in SWB/FE 3147 B/3, 10 February 1998; 'Taiwanese Advisers Meet for First Time', *Jane's Defence Weekly*, 5 August 1998, p. 18.

[88] Sergounin and Subbotin, 'Sino-Russian Military–Technical Cooperation', p. 203; Bruce Hawke, 'Rice Buys Artillery for Myanmar', *Jane's Defence Weekly*, 5 August 1998, p. 19.

[89] DESO, *A Guide to Offset* (London: Ministry of Defence, 1998).

[90] *Ibid.*

[91] Shichor, 'Israel's Military Transfers', p. 83.

[92] Ian Anthony, Susan Eckstein and Jean Pascal Zanders, 'Multilateral Military-Related Export Control Measures', in *SIPRI Yearbook 1997*, pp. 359–63; Alan Osborn, 'Dual-Use Policy in Need of Reform', *Jane's Defence Weekly Defence Industry Report*, August 1998, p. 1.

[93] Michael Binyon, 'Aid Agencies Say Cook Arms Code Is Sham', *The Times*, 16 February 1998; George Parker, 'Ministers "Losing Defence Contracts"', *Financial Times*, 24 July 1998.

[94] Alan Osborn, 'Euro Arms Export Code "Extended"', *Jane's Defence Weekly Defence Industry Report*, October 1998, pp. 1–2.

[95] Martin Walker, 'Anger as Arms Code Is Diluted', *The Guardian*, 26 May 1998, p. 1.

[96] *Ibid.*; Michael Evans, 'Cook Wants EU to Be More Open about Arms Sales', *The Times*, 25 May 1998, p. 1; Lionel Barber and Andrew Parker, 'EU Agrees on Arms Sales Code', *Financial Times*, 26 May 1998, p. 3.

[97] Pamela Pohling-Brown, 'EU Code on Arms Transfers Agreed', *Jane's Defence Weekly*, 3 June 1998, pp. 57–58.

[98] Marc Rogers, 'EU Arms Code Hailed Success as Export Reports "Flood In"', *ibid.*, 7 October 1998, p. 33.

[99] See Malcolm Chalmers, *Confidence-Building in South-East Asia* (Bradford: University of Bradford Department of Peace Studies, 1996); Bates Gill and J. N. Mak (eds), *Arms, Transparency and Security in South-East Asia* (Oxford: Oxford University Press for SIPRI, 1997).

[100] Thayer and Bickers, 'Market Misfire'; 'Currency Crisis Hampers Russian "Arms Assault"', *Bangkok Post*, 2 November 1997; Tim Smart, 'US Arms Makers Feel Pinch in Sales Abroad', *International Herald Tribune*, 27 November 1998.

[101] Damon Bristow, 'Finances Cloud S. E. Asia', *Defense News*, 3 November 1997, p. 19.

[102] Opall, 'Sellers Exercise Flexibility', pp. 1, 20.

[103] Gregor Ferguson and Russ Swinnerton, 'Firms Shift Asia Strategies', *Defense News*, 8 December 1997, p. 1; 'Yarrow-Class Frigates Due Next Year', *Asian Defence Journal*, June 1998, p. 46.

**Chapter 3**

[1] For an overview of the development of China's defence industry, see Arnett, 'Military Technology', pp. 359–86.
[2] Estimates of the size of the Chinese defence industry vary from 1,000 to 50,000 production units employing between three million and 25m workers. See Elisabeth Skons and Bates Gill, 'Arms Production', in *SIPRI Yearbook 1996*, p. 438.
[3] Douglas Barrie, 'Cultural Revolution', *Flight International*, 8 October 1997, p. 36.
[4] Barbara Starr, 'Chinese Modernisation "Efforts" Breach US Law', *Jane's Defence Weekly*, 11 December 1996, p. 11; 'China's Military Use of US Computers Being Checked: Burns', *Straits Times*, 4 July 1997; Stephen Fidler, 'China "Benefited" from Lax US Controls', *Financial Times*, 15 July 1998; Bryan Bender, 'US Export Policy on Satellite Work under Scrutiny', *Jane's Defence Weekly*, 24 June 1998, p. 4.
[5] See Di Hua, 'Threat Perception and Military Planning in China: Domestic Instability and the Importance of Prestige', in Eric Arnett (ed.), *Military Capacity and the Risk of War* (Oxford: Oxford University Press, 1997), pp. 37–38; Michiyo Nakamoto, 'Alarm Bells over China's N-Plans', *Financial Times*, 11 February 1999; Greg Seigle, 'Report to Reveal US Secrets "Stolen" by China', *Jane's Defence Weekly*, 26 May 1999, p. 6.
[6] See Nan Li, 'The PLA's Evolving War-Fighting Doctrine, Strategy and Tactics, 1985–95: A Chinese Perspective', in David Shambaugh and Richard Y. Yang (eds), *China's Military in Transition* (Oxford: Clarendon Press, 1997), p. 184.
[7] See John Frankenstein and Bates Gill, 'Current and Future Challenges Facing Chinese Defence Industries', in Shambaugh and Yang (eds), *China's Military in Transition*, pp. 130–63; John Frankenstein, 'The Peoples Republic of China: Arms Production, Industrial Strategy and Problems of History', in Herbert Wulf (ed.), *Arms Industry Limited* (Oxford: Oxford University Press, 1993); Bates Gill, 'The Impact of Economic Reform on Chinese Defence Industries', in Dimon Liu et al. (eds), *Chinese Military Modernisation* (London: Kegan Paul, 1996).
[8] See Richard Samuels, *Rich Nation, Strong Army: National Security and Technological Transformation of Japan* (Ithaca, NY: Cornell University Press, 1994); Michael Green, *Arming Japan: Defence Production, Alliance Politics and the Postwar Search for Autonomy* (New York: Columbia University Press, 1995).
[9] Arnett, 'Military Research and Development', in *SIPRI Yearbook 1997*, pp. 227–29; *The Military Balance 1998–99*, pp. 15, 167.
[10] US Congress Office of Technology Assessment (OTA), *Global Arms Trade: Commerce in Advanced Military Technology and Weapons* (Washington DC: US Government Printing Office (USGPO), 1991), p. 117.
[11] Peter Atkinson, 'Top 100 Worldwide Defense Firms', *Defense News*, 21 July 1997, p. 6; Paul Lewis, 'FS-Xpensive', *Flight*

*International*, 25 January 1995, p. 27; Andy Chuter, 'Facing the Future', *ibid.*, 16 July 1997, p. 35.

[12] Arnett, 'Military Research and Development', p. 228.

[13] Paul Dibb, *Towards a New Balance of Power in Asia*, Adelphi Paper 295 (Oxford: Oxford University Press for the IISS, 1995), p. 89.

[14] Jon Lake, 'Mitsubishi F-2', *Air International*, March 1997, p. 145.

[15] Charles Smith, 'New World Order, Few Orders: Japan's Arms Makers Feel the Post-Cold War Heat', *Far Eastern Economic Review*, 26 January 1995, p. 54; Barbara Opall, 'Panel Sees Japanese Rebound', *Defense News*, 4 August 1997, p. 8.

[16] Barbara Opall, 'Japanese Push to End Export Ban', *Defense News*, 5 May 1997, pp. 1, 34; 'Japanese Arms-Export Ban May Be Eased', *Jane's Defence Weekly*, 7 January 1998, p. 13.

[17] Arnett, 'Military Research and Development', p. 229; Lewis, 'FS-Xpensive?', p. 27.

[18] Dong Joon Hwang, 'The Role of Defense Industry in Innovation and the Development of Dual-Use Technology', *Korean Journal of Defense Analysis*, vol. 8, no. 1, Summer 1996, p. 161.

[19] Arnett, 'Military Research and Development', p. 232.

[20] Deng Cheng and Michael Chinworth, 'The Teeth of Little Tigers: Offsets, Defence Production and Economic Development in South Korea and Taiwan', in Stephen Martin (ed.), *The Economics of Offsets: Defence Procurement and Countertrade* (Amsterdam: Harwood Economic Publishers, 1996).

[21] Sally Harris, 'South Korea's Military Procurement and Defence Industrialisation', unpublished paper, July 1998.

[22] Paul Lewis, 'Upwardly Mobile', *Flight International*, 23 October 1996, p. 34.

[23] Republic of Korea Ministry of National Defence, *Defense White Paper 1996–1997* (Seoul: Korean Institute for Defense Analyses, 1997), p. 198; US Department of Commerce (DoC), Bureau of Export Administration, Office of Strategic Industries and Economic Strategy, *Pacific Rim Diversification and Defense Market Assessment* (Washington DC: DoC, 1994), p. 95.

[24] Robert Karniol, 'Country Briefing: Taiwan', *Jane's Defence Weekly*, 8 July 1998, p. 26.

[25] Arnett, 'Military Research and Development', p. 235.

[26] Jon Lake, 'AIDC Ching-Kuo: The Indigenous Defence Fighter', *World Air Power Journal*, vol. 26, Autumn 1996, p. 30.

[27] Jon Lake, 'Air Power Analysis: Taiwan', *ibid.*, vol. 33, Summer 1998, p. 146.

[28] Jon Lake, 'Stand Up and Be Strong: Taiwan's Indigenous Trainer', *Air International*, March 1998, pp. 158–64.

[29] Lake, 'AIDC Ching-Kuo', p. 31.

[30] *Ibid.*, p. 40.

[31] Lake, 'Air Power Analysis', p. 150.

[32] See Robert Lowry, *The Armed Forces of Indonesia* (St Leonards, NSW: Allen & Unwin, 1996), pp. 35–38.

[33] Adam Schwarz and Mark Clifford, 'Naval Manoeuvres', *Far Eastern Economic Review*, 13 May 1993, pp. 54–35; John McBeth, 'Techno-Battles', *ibid.*, 7 April 1994, pp. 26–27.

[34] Stephanie Neuman, 'International Stratification and Third World Military Industries', *International Organisation*, vol. 38, no. 1, Winter 1984, pp. 167–97.

[35] See Michael Brzoska and Thomas Ohlson (eds), *Arms Production in the*

*Third World* (London: Taylor &
Francis for SIPRI, 1986); Andrew L.
Ross, 'Full Circle: Conventional
Proliferation, the International
Arms Trade, and Third World Arms
Exports', in Kwang-il Baek, Ronald
D. McLaurin and Chung-in Moon
(eds), *The Dilemma of Third World
Defence Industries: Supplier Control or
Recipient Autonomy?* (Boulder, CO:
Westview Press, 1990).
36 *Country Profile: Indonesia 1995–96*
(London: Economist Intelligence
Unit (EIU), 1996).
37 Dong Joon Hwang, 'The Role of
Defense Industry', p. 157.
38 Janne E. Nolan, *Military Industry
in Taiwan and South Korea* (Basing-
stoke: Macmillan, 1986), pp. 74, 80.
39 'Preparations for Korean Fighter
Project Smooth', *Chungang Ilbo*, 13
August 1994, in FBIS-EAS-94-158,
16 August 1994, pp. 51–52; Karniol,
'Country Briefing: Korea', p. 24.
40 *Countertrade Outlook*, vol. 13, no.
13, 10 July 1995, p. 4.
41 Barbara Opall, 'Taiwan's AIDC
Begins Move Toward
Privatization', *Defense News*, 2
September 1996, p. 36.
42 Singapore Ministry of Defence
spokesman, quoted in Robert
Karniol, 'Country Briefing:
Singapore – State Sector Thrives in
Commercial Arena', *Jane's Defence
Weekly*, 30 April 1997, p. 31.
43 Malaysian Defence Minister
Datuk Seri Syed Hamid Albar,
cited in Robert Karniol, Joris
Janssen Lok and Christopher F.
Foss, 'Malaysian Modernisation',
*ibid.*, 26 November 1997, p. 45.
44 Interview, Jakarta, October 1995.
45 US Government Accounting
Office (USGAO), *Asian Aeronautics*,
GAO/NSIAD-94-140 (Washington
DC: USGPO, 1994), pp. 11–12.
46 See, for example, USGAO,
*Military Exports: Offset Demands
Continue to Grow*, GAO/NSIAD-96-

65 (Washington DC: USGPO, 1996).
47 *Ibid.*, p. 27.
48 Lee Jung-hoon, 'The Missile
Development Race between South
and North Korea, and the US
Policy of Checking', *East Asian
Review*, vol. 9, no. 3, Autumn 1997,
pp. 83–86.
49 'South Korea's K-1/Type 88/K-
1A1 MBT', *Asian Defence Journal*,
January 1998, p. 21.
50 'Asian Airscene', *Air International*,
April 1998, p. 209.
51 Drifte, *The Japanese–Korean High-
Technology Relationship*, pp. 4–6, 18.
52 'Survey: Global Defence
Industry', *The Economist*, 14 June
1997, p. 18.
53 Naoaki Usui, 'JDA Emphasizes
"Revolutionary" Military High
Technology', *Defense News*, 21 July
1997, p. 30.
54 Naoaki Usui, 'Japan Adopts
Acquisition Reform to Cut Costs',
*ibid.*, 15 December 1997, pp. 3, 19.
55 'S. Korea Boosting Dual-Use
Technologies', *Jane's Defence Weekly*,
13 May 1998, p. 131.
56 Frankenstein and Gill, 'Current
and Future Challenges', pp. 153–54.
57 Arnett, 'Military Technology',
p. 369.
58 Barbara Opall, 'Taiwan Trims
Industry Goals', *Defense News*, 1
September 1997, pp. 4, 26.
59 'Dr Tony Tan Sees Scientific
Capability of Defence Science
Organisation', *Media Releases*,
MINDEF Internet Service, 14
March 1997; Karniol, 'Country
Briefing: Singapore', p. 31.
60 OTA, *Building Future Security:
Strategies for Restructuring the
Defence Technology and Industrial
Base* (Washington DC: USGPO,
1992), p. 4.
61 See, for example, Steven Vogel,
'The Power Behind Spin-Ons: The
Military Implications of Japan's
Commercial Technology', in Wayne

Sandholtz *et al.* (eds), *The Highest Stakes: The Economic Foundations of the Next Security System* (Oxford: Oxford University Press, 1992), pp. 55–80.

[62] US Department of Defense, *Key Technologies Plan* (Washington DC: USGPO, 1992).

[63] Len Zuga, 'EW Competition to Surge', *Defense News*, 19 February 1996, p. 20.

[64] Paul Dibb, 'The Revolution in Military Affairs and Asian Security', *Survival*, vol. 39, no. 4, Winter 1997–98, p. 98.

[65] M. Ehsan Ahrari, 'US Military Strategic Perspectives on the PRC', *Asian Survey*, vol. 37, no. 12, December 1997, p. 1,178.

[66] Dibb, 'The Revolution in Military Affairs', p. 103.

[67] Green, *Arming Japan*, p. 4.

[68] 'Survey – Global Defence Industry', p. 18.

[69] Richard Scott, 'South Korea Set for Its First KDX Destroyer', *Jane's Defence Weekly*, 22 July 1998, pp. 23–24.

[70] On the CN-235, see 'BAeA to Help Jakarta Build Maritime Aircraft', *ibid.*, 24 September 1997, p. 12.

[71] Dibb, 'The Revolution in Military Affairs', p. 104.

[72] Paul Lewis, 'All Change in Japan', *Flight International*, 8 February 1998, pp. 34–36.

[73] Lewis, 'Upwardly Mobile', pp. 31–35; Paul Lewis, 'S. Koreans Discuss Link-Up', *ibid.*, 29 January 1997, p. 20; Annabel Wells, 'Compromise and Change', *ibid.*, 21 October 1998, pp. 43–44.

[74] Frankenstein and Gill, 'Current and Future Challenges', pp. 154–56; *China: Arms Control and Disarmament*, p. 15.

[75] Paul Handley, 'Asian Crisis Halts Aerospace Dreams', *Jane's Defence Weekly*, 9 September 1998, p. 44.

[76] 'Singapore Defence Industries Moving Ahead in a Tough Market', *Asian Defence Journal*, December 1994; Karniol, 'State Sector Thrives in Commercial Arena', p. 31.

[77] Paul Lewis, 'ST Aero Will Expand Leasing Business', *Flight International*, 15 January 1997, p. 12; and 'Asian Airscene', *Air International*, vol. 54, no. 4, April 1998, p. 209.

[78] Douglas Barrie, 'AIDC Turns to Civil-Manufacturing Plans', *Flight International*, 20 August 1997, p. 10.

[79] Robert Karniol, 'Country Briefing: Taiwan – Industry Plays Vital Part in Modernisation', *Jane's Defence Weekly*, 8 July 1998, pp. 26–27.

[80] See John Burton, 'Chaebol Fined for Aiding Weaker Units', *Financial Times*, 30 July 1998.

[81] 'Defense Industry for Retooling', *Korea Herald*, 8 July 1998.

[82] Paul Lewis, 'South Korean Trio Start Single Entity Talks', *Flight International*, 21 October 1998, p. 28.

[83] *Yonhap News Agency*, 5 April 1998, in SWB/FE 3194 D/3, 6 April 1998; and 'Foreigners May Buy Defense Firms Freely', *Korea Times*, 20 April 1998.

[84] 'South Korea Seeks Overseas Investment in New Venture', *Flight International*, 30 September 1998, p. 20.

[85] 'Indonesia Agrees to Put Clamps on State Hand-Outs for IPTN', *ibid.*, 21 January 1998, p. 26; 'Habibie Will Let High-Tech Projects Go', *Straits Times*, 16 June 1998.

[86] Sheila McNulty, 'Kuala Lumpur Removes Race-Based Equity Quotas', *Financial Times*, 24 July 1998.

[87] Robert Karniol, 'Boost for Malaysian Competitiveness', *Jane's Defence Weekly*, 11 November 1998, p. 27.

[88] Karniol, 'State Sector Thrives in

Commercial Arena', p. 31.
[89] Karniol, 'Industry Plays Vital Part in Modernisation', pp. 26–27; Lake, 'Air Power Analysis: Taiwan', p. 150.
[90] *The Defence of Thailand 1994* (Bangkok: Ministry of Defence, 1994), pp. 66–67.
[91] 'Post-2000 Delays to China's Arms Goals', *Jane's Defence Weekly*, 21 January 1998, p. 25; 'Survey: Global Defence Industry', p. 20.
[92] 'Industry Embraces Market Reforms', *Jane's Defence Weekly*, 16 December 1998, p. 28.
[93] See Elisabeth Skons, 'Western Europe: Internationalisation of the Arms Industry', in Wulf (ed.), *Arms Industry Limited*, pp. 160–90.
[94] 'Beijing to Open Defence Sector to Foreign Investors', *Straits Times*, 14 July 1997; Paul Beaver, 'China Eyes the West to Finance Defence Growth', *Jane's Defence Weekly*, 23 July 1997, p. 21.
[95] *Ibid.*
[96] 'Lockheed Martin and Mitsubishi to Link in Defence Partnership', *Flight International*, 2 September 1998, p. 10; Richard Bassett, 'Lockheed Tie-Up May Aid Mitsubishi through Economic Crisis', *Jane's Defence Weekly*, 2 September 1998, p. 20.
[97] Richard A. Bitzinger, 'South Korea's Defense Industry at the Crossroads', *Korean Journal of Defense Analysis*, vol. 7, no. 1, Summer 1995, p. 243; 'South Korea's K-1/Type 88/K-1A1 MBT', p. 21; Jason Glashow, 'ROK Threatens Boot for US Aircraft Firm', *Defense News*, 5 February 1996, pp. 1, 37.
[98] 'South Korean Submarine', *Jane's Defence Weekly*, 30 October 1996, p. 17; *Choson Ilbo*, 3 November 1998, in SWB/FE 3381 D/3, 11 November 1998.

[99] Paul Lewis, 'South Korea Selects Radar for KTX-II', *Flight International*, 10 June 1998, p. 21.
[100] 'AIDC and ST Aero in F-5 Upgrade MoU', *Air Forces Monthly*, September 1998, p. 8.
[101] Paul Lewis, 'Singapore Joins Joint Strike Fighter Programme', *Flight International*, 28 April 1999, p. 6; Ramon Lopez, 'Australia Signs for JSF', *ibid.*, 27 May 1998, p. 32.
[102] 'Indonesia Urges Joint Asia-Pacific Arms and Aircraft Industry', *Reuters*, 30 May 1995; Emile John Tan, 'Neighbours, Partners, Friends', *Pioneer*, March 1995, pp. 8–9.
[103] John Burton, 'Fokker Could Be Saviour for Samsung Aerospace', *Financial Times*, 8 February 1996; James Kynge and Gordon Cramb, 'Malaysia Ready to Join Fokker Rescue', *ibid.*, 20 February 1997, p. 34.
[104] Russ Swinnerton, 'Malaysian Firm Sees Growth from Patrol Vessel Program', *Defense News*, 9 June 1997, p. 49.
[105] Paul Lewis, 'Making a Mark', *Flight International*, 21 January 1998, pp. 55–56.
[106] Alan Warnes, 'Malaysia's Military Aerospace Industry', *Air Forces Monthly*, June 1998, pp. 15–17.
[107] *Military Balance 1998/99*, p. 270.
[108] 'Defence Ministry to Replace Foreign Weaponry with Domestic Weapons'; Robert Karniol, 'S. Korea to Build Anti-Ship Missiles', *Jane's Defence Weekly*, 9 December 1998, p. 15.
[109] Robert Karniol, 'Seoul to Buy More F-16s', *Jane's Defence Weekly*, 26 May 1999, p. 14.
[110] *TV3 Television Network*, Kuala Lumpur, 22 January 1998, in SWB/FE 3132 B/6, 23 January 1998.
[111] *Yonhap News Agency*, 9 July 1998, in SWB/FE 3276 D/2, 11 July 1998.

### Chapter 4

[1] The RMA derives from the combination of joint-force doctrines, strategies and tactics, changes in military organisation and integrated logistic support, with advances in intelligence collection, surveillance and reconnaissance (ISR), command, control, communications and computer-processing (C⁴), and precision force. See Joseph S. Nye, Jr., and William A. Owens, 'America's Information Edge', *Foreign Affairs*, vol. 75, no. 2, March–April 1996, pp. 23–24; Dibb, 'The Revolution in Military Affairs and Asian Security', p. 113.

[2] *Ibid.*, pp. 100–104.

[3] See You Ji, 'The PLA's Military Modernisation in the 1990s', in Stuart Harris and Gary Klintworth (eds), *China as a Great Power: Myths, Realities and Challenges in the Asia-Pacific Region* (Melbourne: Longman Australia, 1995), pp. 231–57. On the Chinese navy, see John Downing, 'China's Naval Modernisation', *Jane's Navy International*, May 1998, pp. 16–17; John Downing, 'China's Aircraft Carrier Programme', *Asia-Pacific Defence Reporter*, October–November 1997, p. 6.

[4] See Joseph C. Anselmo, 'China's Military Seeks Great Leap Forward', *Aviation Week and Space Technology*, 12 May 1997, p. 68.

[5] Robert S. Ross, 'China II: Beijing as a Conservative Power', *Foreign Affairs*, vol. 76, no. 2, March–April 1997, pp. 33–34; Stephen Fidler, 'Earliest Date for US Missile Defence System Will Be 2005', *Financial Times*, 21 January 1999.

[6] Stacey Solomon, 'The PLA's Commercial Activities in the Economy: Effects and Consequences', *Issues and Studies*, vol. 31, no. 3, March 1995, pp. 21–43.

[7] See Kensuke Ebata, 'Japan to Receive Four Warships', *Jane's Defence Weekly*, 25 March 1998, p. 13; *Jane's Fighting Ships 1998–99*, p. 377; *Tokyo Shimbun*, 28 April 1995, in FBIS-EAS-95-083, 1 May 1995.

[8] Cloughley, 'Japan Ponders Power Projection', p. 27.

[9] Dibb, 'The Revolution in Military Affairs and Asian Security', p. 110.

[10] Kensuke Ebata and Bryan Bender, 'Japan Takes Delivery of First Boeing 767 AWACS', *Jane's Defence Weekly*, 18 March 1998, p. 17.

[11] 'Japan to Set Up Military Intelligence Agency Next Month', *Straits Times*, 2 December 1996; Carol Reed, 'Japan Gives Go-Ahead to Develop Spy Satellites', *Flight International*, 18 November 1998, p. 30.

[12] Michiyo Nakamoto, 'Japan Moves Closer to Taking Bigger Role in Its Defence', *Financial Times*, 30 April 1999.

[13] Peter Yu Kien-hong, 'Taking Taiwan', *Jane's Intelligence Review*, September 1998, p. 32; Barbara Opall-Rome '... Will Boost C4I Focus, Slow Arms Purchases', *Defense News*, 30 November 1998, p. 4.

[14] 'Taiwanese Satellite Launched', *Jane's Defence Weekly*, 10 February 1999, p. 15.

[15] *Chung Yang Jih Pao*, Taipei, 10 June 1998, in SWB/FE 3256 F/3, 18 June 1998.

[16] *Central News Agency*, 13 April 1998, in SWB/FE 3201 F/4-5, 15 April 1998.

[17] *Ibid.*, 16 June 1998, in SWB/FE 3256 F/3, 18 June 1998.

[18] 'Taiwan to Review Conscription', *Jane's Defence Weekly*, 29 July 1998, p. 17.

[19] Chong-Pin Lin, 'The Military Balance in the Taiwan Straits', in Shambaugh and Yang (eds), *China's Military in Transition*, p. 327.

[20] *Ibid.*

[21] *Ibid.*, pp. 329–30.

[22] *Lien Ho Pao*, Taipei, 11 February 1999, in SWB/FE 3459 F/2, 15 February 1999; 'Taiwan Deploys Missiles to Protect Capital', *Washington Times*, 28 August 1998, p. A15.

[23] *Jane's Fighting Ships 1998–99*, p. 405.

[24] Republic of Korea Ministry of National Defence, *Defense White Paper 1996–1997*, p. 103.

[25] Robert Karniol, 'RoK Plans Its First Military Satellite Launch for 2005', *Jane's Defence Weekly*, 11 November 1998, p. 19.

[26] *Korea Times*, 21 February 1995, in FBIS-EAS-95-036, 23 February 1995. See also Prasun K. Sengupta, 'The Republic of Korea Armed Forces at 50', *Asian Defence Journal*, October 1998, pp. 10, 12.

[27] *Hanguk Ilbo*, Seoul, 3 October 1994, in FBIS-EAS-94-192, 4 October 1994; Steve Glain, 'South Korea's Army Battles a Breakdown in Discipline', *Asian Wall Street Journal*, 7 December 1994.

[28] See Brian Cloughley, 'Korean Flashpoint Waits to Be Ignited', *Jane's International Defense Review*, September 1996, pp. 27–28, 31–32.

[29] 'Singapore Puts Force Integration into Place', *Jane's Defence Weekly*, 30 April 1997, pp. 25–29; Robert Karniol, 'Singapore Edges Closer to Satellite Reality', *ibid.*, 28 April 1999, p. 14.

[30] 'Singapore Link 16 Move Angers US', *Flight International*, 24 February 1999, p. 6.

[31] 'Special Report: US Military Presence in Asia', *Asian Defence Journal*, January–February 1999, p. 58.

[32] Gary K. Bertsch, Richard T. Cupitt and Takehiko Yamamoto, 'Trade, Export Controls, and Non-Proliferation in the Asia Pacific Region', *Pacific Review*, vol. 10, no. 3, 1997, p. 423.

[33] *Yonhap News Agency*, 10 August 1998, in SWB/FE 3303 D/4, 12 August 1998; *Central News Agency*, 20 July 1998, in SWB/FE 3285 F/2, 22 July 1998.

[34] Shawn Crispin and Shim Jae Hoon, 'Buying Time', *Far Eastern Economic Review*, 1 April 1999, pp. 18–20.

[35] *Kyodo News Service*, 15 December 1997, in SWB/FE 3105 D/2, 18 December 1997.

[36] Bill Gertz, 'Pentagon: N. Korea's Missiles Operational', *Washington Times*, 10 June 1998.

[37] Joseph S. Bermudez, 'Taepo-dong Launch Brings DPRK Missiles Back into the Spotlight', *Jane's Intelligence Review*, October 1998, pp. 30–32.

[38] 'N. Korea "Building Missile Launch Sites"', *Straits Times*, 9 December 1998.

[39] Dennis M. Gormley, 'Hedging Against the Cruise-Missile Threat', *Survival*, vol. 40, no. 1, Spring 1998, p. 97.

[40] 'North Korea Can Strike America?', *Asian Defence Journal*, November 1995, p. 75; Barbara Starr, 'North Korea Redeploys Aircraft Closer to DMZ', *Jane's Defence Weekly*, 3 April 1996, p. 3; 'On the Way: N. Korean Missile that Could Hit US', *Straits Times*, 21 September 1997; 'North Korean Missile Threat to USA', *Jane's Defence Weekly*, 10 March 1999, p. 17.

[41] Alastair Iain Johnston, 'Prospects for Chinese Nuclear Force Modernization: Limited Deterrence Versus Multilateral Arms Control', in Shambaugh and Yang (eds), *China's Military in Transition*, pp. 285–94.

[42] *Ibid.*, pp. 298–99; Lin, 'The Military Balance in the Taiwan Straits', pp. 326–27; Nigel Holloway, 'Cruise Control', *Far Eastern Economic Review*, 14 August

1997, pp. 14–16; Nigel Holloway, 'Touchy Issue', *ibid.*, 23 October 1997, pp. 29–30; Gormley, 'Hedging Against the Cruise-Missile Threat', pp. 99–100; John Downing, 'China Develops Cruise Missiles', *Asia-Pacific Defence Reporter*, August–September 1997, p. 6; Paul Beaver, 'China Prepares to Field New Missile', *Jane's Defence Weekly*, 24 February 1999, p. 3.

[43] Tony Walker and Stephen Fidler, 'China Builds Up Missile Threat', *Financial Times*, 10 February 1999; Tony Walker, Stephen Fidler and Mure Dicke, 'New Missiles Raise Taiwan Strait Tensions', *ibid.*, 12 March 1999.

[44] Bryan Bender, 'USA Keeps to NMD Plan', *Jane's Defence Weekly*, 2 September 1998, p. 11.

[45] Susan V. Lawrence, 'Miles to Go', *Far Eastern Economic Review*, 26 November 1998, p. 24.

[46] *Yomiuri Shimbun*, 2 September 1998.

[47] Barbara Opall-Rome, 'Taiwan Resists Call to Embrace TMD', *Defense News*, 30 November 1998, p. 4.

[48] '10-Year Taiwan Arms Plan to Counter China', *Straits Times*, 13 July 1998; John Pomfret, 'Taiwanese Seek US Destroyers', *Washington Post*, 2 December 1998, p. 3; Barbara Opall, 'US Readies $1.7 Billion Package for Taiwan', *Defense News*, 3 May 1999, p. 1.

[49] 'S. Korea Refuses Participation in TMD', *Jane's Defence Weekly*, 17 March 1999, p. 16; Robert Karniol, 'South Korea May Attract M-SAM Radar Work Soon', *ibid.*, 26 May 1999, p. 14.

[50] See Michael Pillsbury (ed.), *Chinese Views of Future Warfare* (Washington DC: National Defense University Press, 1997).

[51] Gao Heng, 'Future Military Trends', *ibid.*, p. 94.

[52] Solomon M. Karmel, 'The Maoist Drag on China's Military', *Orbis*, vol. 42, no. 3, Summer 1998, pp. 375–86.

[53] Robert Garland, '*Rosvooruzheniye* and the Russian Arms Industry – A Missed Opportunity?', *RUSI Newsbrief*, vol. 18, no. 7, July 1998, pp. 55–56.

[54] Lin, 'The Military Balance in the Taiwan Straits', p. 327.

[55] See Arnett, 'Military Technology', pp. 367–71; Nigel Holloway, 'Revolutionary Defence', *Far Eastern Economic Review*, 24 July 1997, p. 25.

[56] Mark A. Stokes, 'China's Strategic Modernisation: Implications for US National Security', Research Project under the US Air Force (USAF) Institute for Security Studies, October 1997, p. 11.

[57] John Pomfret, 'US Companies Prepare for End of Ban on Weapons Sales to China', *International Herald Tribune*, 25 May 1998; 'Taipei Seeks US Weapons to Keep Balance of Power', *Straits Times*, 13 July 1998, p. 12.

[58] Clifford Beal, 'China Shows New AWACS-Killer Missile', *Jane's Defence Weekly*, 16 September 1998, p. 13; 'China Raises Arms Muscle with Anti-Radar Missile Work', *ibid.*, 23 September 1998, p. 15; Paul Beaver, 'China Develops Anti-Satellite Laser System', *ibid.*, 2 December 1998, p. 18.